CW00509777

My name is Latoyah, and I am the creator
popular food, healthy recipes and

I have always loved to cook and experiment with different
flavours and ideas in the kitchen, especially when it comes to
making meals that are both healthy and delicious. For years I
would play around with flavour combinations and new dishes,
but never wrote them down or saved them. This meant when I
tried to recreate them, I could never fully remember all the
processes and ingredients.

5 years ago I decided to start posting my recipes and ideas in an
online space, so that I could refer to them and share them with
friends and family.

Since then I have gained tens of thousands of followers across
social media, and millions of views on my website. After getting
requests daily to bring out my own cookbook, I decided to take
matters into my own hands and get writing!

This book is entirely self-written and self-published using real
pictures of the meals I have made and eaten and photographed
myself in my own kitchen!

Thank you for your support in purchasing this book.

Search 'Sugar Pink Food' to visit my blog online.

Contents

Breakfast

Lunch

Dinner

Dinner

Dinner

Sides

Notes & Information

All nutritional values have been calculated using Very Well Fit to analyze the ingredients. They are for guidance only, and it is always recommended to double check if you are following a calorie specific diet.

All recipes are copyright of Sugar Pink Food and should not be photographed, copied or shared anywhere.

Recipes are made using low fat meat, low sugar content and as few calories as possible.

For more information about Sugar Pink Food, please visit www.latoyah.co.uk Please email SugarPinkFood@gmail.com if you have any questions or comments.

This book is not associated with any diet club.

Recipes are made using a fan oven. See conversion chart below.

Gas Mark	° Celsius	° Celsius Fan	° Fahrenheit
¼	110°c	100°c	225°F
½	130°c	120°c	250°F
1	140°c	130°c	275°F
2	150°c	140°c	300°F
3	170°c	155°c	325°F
4	180°c	165°c	350°F
5	190°c	180°c	375°F
6	200°c	190°c	400°F
7	220°c	200°c	425°F
8	230°c	210°c	450°F
9	240°c	220°c	475°F

Tips For Healthy Eating

Low fat meat

An easy way to reduce your fat intake, is to reduce the amount of fatty meat that you eat. Try switching regular minced beef to 5% fat beef mince. Instead of eating fatty bacon, try bacon medallions, or trim any fat off the rashers yourself. Chicken and turkey are both lean meats that are also incredibly versatile.

Cut out cooking with oil

I always try and avoid cooking with excess oil. I recommend investing in good quality non-stick pans, so that you can fry off your food without having to grease the pan. There are also plenty of low calorie cooking sprays on offer.

Increase fruit and veg intake

Fruit and vegetables are a good source of vitamins and minerals. They are also an excellent source of dietary fibre, which can help to maintain a healthy gut and prevent constipation and other digestive problems. I always try to fill up on fruit and veg when I need something to snack on.

Reduce sugar intake

Sugar is one of the biggest causes of weight gain. If buying pre-made or processed food, always check the amount of sugar it contains, as you may be surprised! Cut out sugary drinks, sugar in your tea, and sugary snacks like chocolate bars and sweets.

Make sure you eat a healthy breakfast

For years I was guilty of not eating a proper breakfast in the morning, thinking I was saving calories. Eating breakfast actually kick-starts your metabolism, helping you burn calories throughout the day.

BREAKFAST RECIPES

SLOW COOKER SHAKSHUKA

PREP TIME
10 minutes

COOK TIME
3 hours

READY IN
3 hours 10

SERVINGS
4 servings

CALORIES
390 Kcal serving

SOURCE
Sugar Pink Food

Ingredients

1 large red onion, diced
1 red and 1 yellow pepper, diced
a pinch sea salt and black pepper
1 oxo cube, crumbled up
3 cloves garlic, pressed or minced
2tbsp tomato paste
1tsp ground cumin
2tsp smoked paprika
1 tin of chopped tomatoes
1 carton of passata
1 egg per person
a handful of crumbled up feta
a few slices of chorizo, chopped

Steps

Add everything except the eggs and feta to your slow cooker.

Mix everything together well and set on low for 6 hours, or high for 3 hours.

You can either add pre-poached eggs to the sauce, or crack your eggs into the mix in the slow cooker and leave for 3 minutes.

Serve with crumbled up feta on top with some bread!

Notes

A Shakshuka is a Middle Eastern and North African dish made of a hearty, spiced tomato and pepper sauce topped with a poached egg and feta. I first had one at a restaurant, and wanted to make one myself ever since.

SLOW COOKER SHAKSHUKA

I love any food that is easy to make, and this one doesn't get much easier! You can literally throw all of the ingredients into your slow cooker, leave overnight, and it will be ready for you in the morning.

You can experiment by adding different flavours, leaving out the meat, or even adding more!

You can add the egg in at the end to cook in the sauce, or if you find it easier you can poach the egg and then add it in when ready to serve.

CHILLI CHEESE OMELETTES

PREP TIME
10 minutes

COOK TIME
10 minutes

READY IN
20 minutes

SERVINGS
2 servings

CALORIES
211 Kcal serving

SOURCE
Sugar Pink Food

Ingredients

3 eggs

½ onion, finely diced

½ chilli, finely diced

a pinch of salt and pepper

a pinch of smoked paprika

low calorie cooking spray

40g cheese per person

Steps

Spray the waffle iron with low calorie cooking spray.

Switch it on and allow it to heat up.

Meanwhile, crack the eggs into a bowl. Mix with all the ingredients.

When the irons have warmed up, pour in the egg mixture and close.

Cook for 2 minutes and check. Continue to cook until golden brown and cooked all the way through.

Serve with salad and sprinkle with any left over chilli.

Notes

I was lucky enough to get a waffle iron for Christmas last year, and I absolutely love it. I don't think I have ever used it for actual waffle batter, but it is so versatile that I have found many uses for it.

MAGIC OAT PANCAKES

PREP TIME
10 minutes

COOK TIME
5 minutes

READY IN
15 minutes

SERVINGS
6 Pancakes

CALORIES
169 Kcal per 3

SOURCE
Sugar Pink Food

Ingredients

2 eggs

40g porridge oats

4tbsp fat free Greek yogurt

1tbsp sweetener

½tsp vanilla extract

Steps

Separate the egg whites from the yolks, and put in separate bowls. Whisk the egg whites until light and fluffy, forming soft peaks.

Blend the oats up in a blender until smooth.

Mix the egg yolks, yogurt, sweetener and vanilla extract.

Fold in the egg whites and stir to form the pancake batter.

Heat a frying pan and spray with Frylight, add a dollop of mixture to the middle of the pan.

Cook for 2 minutes, then use a spatula to flip the pancake over. Repeat until the mixture has gone.

Notes

Simple, easy, lower calorie pancakes that are perfect for lower calorie breakfasts.

STEAK & EGG TRAYBAKE

PREP TIME
10 minutes

COOK TIME
10 minutes

READY IN
20 minutes

SERVINGS
2 servings

CALORIES
387 Kcal portion

SOURCE
Sugar Pink Food

Ingredients

2 large 'minute steaks' or 'sizzle steaks' (thin steaks that cook quickly)

½ red pepper, finely chopped

½ yellow pepper, finely chopped

1 large potato, finely chopped into cubes

½tsp smoked paprika

1tbsp Worcestershire sauce

Salt and pepper

low calorie cooking spray

2 eggs

Steps

Preheat the oven to 180°C.

Add potatoes to the tray, sprinkle with salt and pepper, and spray with low calorie cooking spray. Bake for 10 minutes.

Meanwhile, slice the steak and sprinkle with smoked paprika.

Remove the potatoes from the oven, then add the steak and peppers to the dish.

Create 2 spaces for the egg, then crack the egg into the wells.

Bake in the oven for 10 minutes.

Notes

A tasty breakfast of eggs, steak, potatoes and vegetables. Even easier to prepare as you add all the ingredients into one tray to cook.

VANILLA OAT WAFFLE PANCAKES

PREP TIME
10 minutes

COOK TIME
20 minutes

READY IN
30 minutes

SERVINGS
1 serving

CALORIES
316 Kcal

SOURCE
Sugar Pink Food

Ingredients

1 large egg

40g oats

½ tbsp granulated sweetener

175g fat free natural yogurt

1 tsp vanilla extract

To top:

fruit and sugar free syrup of your choice.

Steps

Blitz all of the ingredients in a blender. Mix until smooth.

Add mix to the waffle maker, and cook until golden brown.

If using a waffle mould, bake in the oven at 120°C for 20 minutes, or until golden.

Top with fruit of your choice.

Notes
I do love sweet waffles, and thanks to blitzing up some oats, these sweet vanilla waffles are super fluffy, delicious and slimming friendly.

CHEESE & BACON SOLDIERS

PREP TIME
10 minutes

COOK TIME
10 minutes

READY IN
20 minutes

SERVINGS
2 servings

CALORIES
320 Kcal serving

SOURCE
Sugar Pink Food

Ingredients

1 Schär gluten free white ciabatta

40g extra light cheese

1 bacon medallion, cut into small pieces

1 cooked boiled egg

Steps

Slice the ciabatta lengthways into long slices, and then cut each of those slices in half to create long soldiers.

Meanwhile, fry-off the small bacon pieces in low calorie cooking spray. Cook until dark and crispy, or however you prefer.

Spray the soldiers with low calorie cooking spray, and then place them under the grill. Grill on each side for 2 minutes.

Top with cheese and bacon, then place back under the grill for the cheese to melt.

Notes

If you love dippy eggs and soldiers, then this dish is for you! Take your soldiers to the next level, by topping them with cheese and crispy bacon.

CHEESE & BACON SOLDIERS

I wouldn't really call this a recipe, more a simple method to make a delicious breakfast!

For the bacon bits, I just fry off some bacon medallions and then cut them up into small chunks to put on top of the soldiers.

A breakfast of champions!

BAKED OATS

PREP TIME
5 minutes

COOK TIME
30 minutes

READY IN
35 minutes

SERVINGS
2 servings

CALORIES
205 Kcal serving

SOURCE
Sugar Pink Food

Ingredients

40g of porridge oats

1 large egg

½tsp of vanilla extract

½tsp of baking powder

1 fat free vanilla yogurt pot

1tbsp sweetener

fresh strawberries, raspberries, blueberries and a custard yogurt

Steps

Preheat the oven to 200°C.

Spray foil container with Frylight.

Add all the ingredients, and mix together to combine.

Bake in the oven for 30 minutes until golden.

Add the fruit to serve.

Notes
This is a super basic baked oats recipe, and you can really experiment with different fruits and flavours. Serve it with plenty of fruit to make it extra filling!

FULLY LOADED HASH BROWN WAFFLES

PREP TIME
10 minutes

COOK TIME
15 minutes

READY IN
25 minutes

SERVINGS
2 servings

CALORIES
559 Kcal serving

SOURCE
Sugar Pink Food

Ingredients

2 large potatoes

1tsp minced garlic

a pinch salt and pepper

1tsp smoked paprika

1 egg lightly beaten

4 bacon medallions

2 eggs, for poaching

40g extra light cheese per person

chopped cherry tomatoes

Steps

Preheat the waffle iron as per manufacturer's instructions.

Peel the potatoes and grate until they are all shredded. Place the shredded potatoes in a tea towel, then wrap the tea towel around. Squeeze out all the excess moisture in the potatoes over the sink through the tea towel.

Transfer to a bowl and add the beaten egg, salt, pepper, garlic, smoked paprika and mix well. Divide the mixture into 2. Place half the mixture in the waffle iron. Cook for approximately 8 minutes, until crispy and golden.

Meanwhile, chop the bacon into slices and fry-off in a pan sprayed with Frylight. Poach the eggs just before serving.

Top the hash brown waffles with bacon, eggs, tomatoes and cheese!

Notes

Another great waffle iron recipe! Alternatively, you can get a waffle mould for pretty cheap online, the just oven bake instead in a medium heat until golden.

FULLY LOADED HASH BROWN WAFFLES

There's nothing better than a proper hearty weekend breakfast! This recipe is what I came up with after just trying out my waffle iron a few times.

The hash brown waffles are topped with bacon, tomatoes, cheese and a poached egg, but you can add any toppings you fancy!

CREAMY GARLIC MUSHROOMS

PREP TIME
10 minutes

COOK TIME
10 minutes

READY IN
20 minutes

SERVINGS
2 servings

CALORIES
200 Kcal serving

SOURCE
Sugar Pink Food

Ingredients

225g mushrooms

2 cloves of garlic, minced

1tbsp of Quark, fat free cream cheese.

1tsp dried mixed herbs, like basil or parsley

salt and pepper to taste

low calorie cooking spray

To serve: 2 slices of 400g wholemeal toast per person

poached egg

Steps

Heat a frying pan over a medium heat.

Add mushrooms and stir until they soften, moving them around the pan throughout to avoid sticking.

Add the garlic, herbs, salt and pepper, and stir well.

Turn the heat down to low, then add the cream cheese and mix well. You may need to add a little more Quark if the mushrooms aren't fully covered.

Notes

This is a delicious recipe that is perfect for breakfast, lunch or brunch! Creamy garlic mushrooms on top of wholemeal toast. This recipe is low in fat, low in calories and also vegetarian.

ONE PAN BREAKFAST

PREP TIME
10 minutes

COOK TIME
10 minutes

READY IN
20 minutes

SERVINGS
2

CALORIES
518 Kcal serving

SOURCE
Sugar Pink Food

Ingredients

2 large potatoes, cut into small cubes

½ onion, finely diced

½ garlic clove, crushed

½ tin of beans

a handful of mushrooms, sliced

2 bacon medallions, sliced, all fat removed

35g feta cheese, crumbled

low calorie cooking spray

pinch of salt and pepper

pinch of smoked paprika

1 egg

Steps

Spray a frying pan with low calorie cooking spray.

Add the potatoes and fry in the pan for 10 minutes, stirring constantly to avoid them burning. When cooked, remove from the pan and set aside.

Add the mushrooms, onions, garlic, salt, pepper and smoked paprika. Stir and mix well. Simmer over a low heat for 2 minutes, or until the mushrooms are cooked.

Add the beans and cooked potatoes to the pan and mix well.

Make a gap for the egg, and crack into the gap. Cover the pan and leave for 3 minutes, or until the egg looks cooked through.

Crumble with feta on top and serve!

Notes

I used a relatively small pan, and could only fit the 1 egg in, which made it a perfect size for 1 person. Just adjust the amount of potatoes and the egg if you are making this for more people.

ONE PAN BREAKFAST

I use a frying pan to cook all the ingredients together, then add the egg and cover the pan so it cooks all the way through. If you have an airfryer, you can cook the potatoes up in that first, then add them in just before cooking the egg.

You can experiment with this dish, and add as many different low fat ingredients to make it as tasty and as filling as possible.

BAKED HASH BROWNS

PREP TIME
10 minutes

COOK TIME
25 minutes

READY IN
35 minutes

SERVINGS
6 hash browns

CALORIES
63 Kcal per hash

SOURCE
Sugar Pink Food

Ingredients

2 medium potatoes, peeled and grated

1 egg, beaten

1 tsp salt

½ tsp chilli powder

½ tsp dried basil

¼ tsp ground cumin

¼ tsp black pepper

½ tsp smoked paprika

½ tsp onion powder

low calorie cooking spray

Steps

Preheat the oven to 180°C.

Using a clean tea towel, add the shredded potato in the middle of it. Squeeze all the liquid out of the potatoes using the tea towel. This is what gives them the crispiness.

Remove from the tea towel, place in a bowl and add the rest of the ingredients. Mix well.

Spray a muffin tin with low calorie cooking spray.

Add about 1 tbsp of the potato mixture into each muffin tin. Use the back of the spoon to press down the mixture until it is flat on top and fully pushed into each muffin tin hole.

Bake in the oven for 20 minutes, or until golden and crispy.

Notes
These hash browns are made using a muffin tin to get the perfect shape and crispiness.

EGG IN HOLE

PREP TIME
5 minutes

COOK TIME
10 minutes

READY IN
15 minutes

SERVINGS
2 people

CALORIES
198 Kcal per slice

SOURCE
Sugar Pink Food

Ingredients

2 slices 400g wholemeal bread

2 eggs

½ onion, finely diced

1 tomato, finely chopped

½ red pepper, finely chopped

½ garlic clove

pinch of salt and pepper

Steps

Cut a hole in the centre of each slice. Remove the middle.

Fry-off the vegetables in a frying pan

Bunch the vegetables into the centre of the pan, then place the bread over the top.

Whisk the eggs, add the salt and pepper, then pour into the whole.

Pin on Pinterest

Place the bread insides on the top of the egg. Cook for 2 minutes, then flip the bread over.

Keep repeating until the egg is cooked through and the bread is crispy.

Notes

This method means that I pack in some extra veggies with my meal as well.
Usually an egg in hole recipe is done with a fried egg, but me being me wanted
to be a little different!

BREAKFAST TOWER STACK

PREP TIME
10 minutes

COOK TIME
10 minutes

READY IN
20 minutes

SERVINGS
2 stacks

CALORIES
275 Kcal each

SOURCE
Sugar Pink Food

Ingredients

2 potato waffles

2 rashers of bacon, all fat removed

½ tin beans

a few mushrooms

1 egg for poaching

Steps

Cook the potato waffles as per pack instructions.

Spray a low calorie cooking spray in a frying pan and heat over a medium heat.

Fry-off the bacon and mushrooms.

Cook the beans as per tin instructions.

Meanwhile, poach the egg.

When the waffles are cooked, stack the potato waffles, beans, and mushrooms.

Top with the poached egg.

Notes
A proper quick and super simple breakfast that you can throw together in the morning. I used ready made waffles for extra ease.

BISCOFF BAKED OATS

PREP TIME
10 minutes

COOK TIME
35 minutes

READY IN
45 minutes

SERVINGS
4 Squares

CALORIES
229 Kcal each

SOURCE
Sugar Pink Food

Ingredients

160g of porridge oats

2tsp ground cinnamon

¼tsp ground nutmeg

¼tsp ground ginger

¼tsp ground allspice

¼tsp ground cloves

1½tbsp of sweetner

1 egg

1½cups milk

Steps

Line a tin approximately 27cm x 20cm with baking paper. Preheat the oven to 180°C, 160°C fan oven.

Add the porridge oats to a bowl.

Add the cinnamon, nutmeg, ginger, allspice, cloves and sweetener, mix well.

Mix the sweetener, oat milk (or cows milk) and flax egg (or egg) in a bowl and whisk. Add this to the oats and mix well. Add more oat milk if the mix looks too sticky.

Add mixture to the lined tin and bake for 35 minutes until golden like a flapjack.

Serve with fruit and a teaspoon of melted lotus spread drizzled on top. and add a Biscoff Biscuit for extra deliciousness!

Notes
They are a delicious breakfast treat, and the beauty of these oats is that you can make a larger batch and portion it up, so you always have some ready in the morning.

SIMPLE & EASY BREAKFAST IDEAS

These breakfast ideas are so simple, they don't require a recipe!

Poached Egg on Toast

A super simple meal that's easy to get together. Use wholemeal bread for extra fibre, and fresh eggs to make poaching easier. Serve with extra vegetables, like spinach or mushrooms.

Fruit, Yoghurt & Oats

This is one of my favourite breakfasts to take to work! Fresh fruit with some fat free yoghurt and porridge oats for fibre.

Beans on Wholemeal Toast

Beans are another great source of fibre, and are delicious on wholemeal toast with a bit of cheese.

Scrambled Egg on Toast with Tomatoes

If poached eggs aren't for you, try some scrambled eggs with fresh tomatoes. The more vegetables you can get on your plate, the better! It's both filling and good for you.

Bacon wrapped Asparagus

A tasty, low carb breakfast. Just take some fat free bacon medallions and wrap them around some asparagus tips, then oven bake. They are even better when dipped into a runny egg!

LUNCH RECIPES

CHICKEN & BACON CLUB SANDWICH

PREP TIME
10 minutes

COOK TIME
5 minutes

READY IN
15 minutes

SERVINGS
`1 sandwich

CALORIES
357 Kcal sandwich

SOURCE
Sugar Pink Food

Ingredients

3 slices 400g wholemeal bread

cooked chicken

2 cooked bacon medallions, all fat removed

½ tsp extra light mayo

½ tsp yellow mustard

40g extra light cheese, sliced

a handful of mixed salad

Steps

Lightly toast the 3 slices of bread.

Lay the 3 slices out next to each other.

Add mayo to the first slice, and mustard to the second slice.

Add salad on top of the mustard, then add the cheese slices and bacon on top of that.

Place the third slice on top to make the first layer of sandwich.

Layer the chicken, cheese and salad on top of that sandwich, then top it off with the mayo slice

Notes

A club sandwich is one of those Instagrammable, 3 layer sandwiches. It's usually filled with cooked meats, mayo and salad.

CHICKEN & BACON CLUB SANDWICH

I wanted to make a version of this that is as healthy and low in calories as possible.

I used wholemeal bread, extra light cheese and extra light mayo. I also added a small amount of mustard for an extra kick.

Just cut the crusts off the bread to allow for the 3 slices of bread, and toast the slices of bread before constructing the sandwich.

SWEET POTATO & CARROT SOUP

PREP TIME
10 minutes

COOK TIME
45 minutes

READY IN
35 minutes

SERVINGS
4 servings

CALORIES
218 Kcal serving

SOURCE
Sugar Pink Food

Ingredients

100ml fat free fromage frais, plus extra to serve

500g sweet potatoes, peeled and cut into chunks

300g carrots, peeled and cut into chunks

salt and pepper

2 onions, finely chopped

2 garlic cloves, crushed

1l vegetable stock

Steps

Heat oven to 200°C.

Add sweet potatoes, carrots and garlic cloves into a large roasting tin.

Spray vegetables with low calorie cooking spray. Roast the vegetables in the oven for 30 minutes.

Meanwhile, in a saucepan fry the onions. Add the stock and simmer for 5-10 minutes until the onions are soft.

Once the roasted vegetables are done, remove from the oven and leave to cool. Pull out the garlic cloves and squeeze out the garlic paste, discarding the skins. Add the vegetable mix to a saucepan with the stock and use a hand blender to blitz until smooth.

Add salt and pepper, and stir through the fromage frais until smooth. Add more stock to thin down if needed.

Notes

This is a really delicious and super easy recipe, perfect for autumn. I roasted all the vegetables to get loads of flavour and then blended until smooth.

ITALIAN PASTA SALAD

PREP TIME
10 minutes

COOK TIME
30 minutes

READY IN
40 minutes

SERVINGS
4 servings

CALORIES
583 Kcal serving

SOURCE
Sugar Pink Food

Ingredients

150g dried pasta bows

2 cooked chicken breasts, shredded or cubed

½ cucumber, diced

1 handful halved cherry tomatoes

4 bacon medallions, all fat removed

¼ cup chopped fresh flat-leaf parsley

2tbsp cider vinegar

2tbsp balsamic vinegar

a few lettuce leaves, sliced into strips

olive oil light cooking spray

Optional: 90g feta cheese

Steps

Boil the pasta in salted water until pasta is soft.

Drain the pasta, then rinse in cold water to cool.

In a large bowl add the chicken, cucumber, tomatoes, bacon, parsley, and lettuce. Mix together.

Top with the cool pasta, vinegars and season with salt and pepper. Spray with a few squirts of olive oil cooking spray and mix everything up to get an even coating on all the ingredients.

Split into separate servings ready for lunches, and top with 30g feta per serving if using the feta as a healthy extra.

Notes

This is a really simple dish to pull together and works perfectly for 'take to work' lunches. You can use any type of pasta, but I'm very fond of pasta bows!

PIZZA HASSELBACK POTATOES

PREP TIME
10 minutes

COOK TIME
45 minutes

READY IN
55 minutes

SERVINGS
1-2 people

CALORIES
348 Kcal serving

SOURCE
Sugar Pink Food

Ingredients

2 medium baking potatoes

salt and ground pepper

low calorie cooking spray

3 slices of salami per potato, each slice halved

80g extra light cheese, split into 2 piles of 40g

For the sauce:

4tbsp passata

A pinch salt and pepper

1tsp Italian herbs

Steps

Preheat the oven to 200°C.

Slice the potatoes across at about a cm thickness or as thin as you can. (If the potato is placed in a large spoon the edges of the spoon will prevent you from slicing clear through the potato).

Spray the potatoes with Frylight and massage into the skin. Place on a baking tray and cook for 15 minutes. Meanwhile, mix up the pizza sauce.

Remove the potatoes from the oven and allow to cook to the point you can handle touching them. Put a knife in the slices and spread them open. Insert a few slices of salami into the gaps. I cut each salami slice in half, so that I can put more slices in the gaps. Top the potatoes with the pizza sauce and then the cheese.

Bake in the oven for 30 minutes, until the potatoes are cooked through and the cheese has melted.

Notes

Hasselback potatoes are a simple dish - whole potatoes cut to resemble a fan or accordion when roasted.

CREAM OF TOMATO SOUP

PREP TIME
10 minutes

COOK TIME
20 minutes

READY IN
30 minutes

SERVINGS
4 servings

CALORIES
116 Kcal serving

SOURCE
Sugar Pink Food

Ingredients

2 tins of chopped tomatoes

1 tin of baked beans

4 small pickled onions (or one large one), chopped in half

½ pint vegetable stock

a pinch of salt and pepper

1tsp Worcestershire shire sauce

½tsp sweetener

Steps

Put all ingredients in a large saucepan and bring to the boil.

As soon as the soup boils, reduce the heat to the lowest and allow to simmer.

Cover and leave for 15 minutes to simmer gently.

Once cooled slightly, add to a blender and blitz until the mixture is completely smooth.

Can be kept in the fridge in a sealed container for up to one week.

Notes

This is a really simple dish to pull together and works perfectly for 'take to work' lunches.

MUSHROOM PÂTÉ

PREP TIME
10 minutes

COOK TIME
10 minutes

READY IN
20 minutes

SERVINGS
4 servings

CALORIES
66 Kcal serving

SOURCE
Sugar Pink Food

Ingredients

1 medium onion, finely chopped

low calorie cooking spray

1 garlic clove, crushed

120g mushrooms, finely chopped

100g chestnut mushrooms, finely chopped

3tsp chopped fresh tarragon

113g Quark

salt and freshly ground black pepper

Steps

Fry the onions in low calorie spray until softened. Add the garlic and cook until everything is beginning to brown.

Add the mushrooms and cook for 6-7 minutes, Remove the pan from the heat and leave to cool completely.

Put the Quark, mushroom mixture and seasoning into a blender or food processor with the tarragon and blend until smooth.

Line a dish with cling film and pour the mixture in, spread evenly.

Chill in the refrigerator to set for a while.

Notes

This is a great recipe for mushroom pâté that's easy to make, as well as delicious

MUSHROOM PÂTÉ

A delicious, light, veggie pâté.

I love this as an alternative to butter on my toast, with a lovely, runny poached egg on top!

You can keep it sealed in the fridge for up to a week after you have made it.

BLT PASTA SALAD

PREP TIME
10 minutes

COOK TIME
10 minutes

READY IN
30 minutes

SERVINGS
4 servings

CALORIES
324 Kcal serving

SOURCE
Sugar Pink Food

Ingredients

1tbsp olive oil

1tbsp wholegrain mustard

2tbsp balsamic vinegar

salt and freshly ground black pepper

½ small clove of garlic, minced or very finely chopped

300g dried pasta shells or bows

10 slices bacon, all visible fat removed, and cooked

a large handful of cherry tomatoes, diced

½ iceberg lettuce, finely chopped

Steps

Cook the pasta according to the instructions.

Meanwhile, in a small bowl, make the vinaigrette by whisking together the olive oil, mustard, balsamic, salt, pepper and garlic.

Once the pasta is cooked, drain and set aside to cool for 10 minutes. Once cooled, mix in with the vinaigrette. If you are serving straight away mix the bacon, lettuce and tomato together with the pasta. If, like me, you want to take this to work throughout the week, store the bacon, lettuce and tomato separately in a sealed container. This keeps everything fresh. Mix together with the pasta once you are ready to serve

Notes

Take the delicious combination of bacon, lettuce and tomato and instead of slapping it between 2 pieces of white bread, mix with pasta and a delicious balsamic and wholegrain mustard vinaigrette.

BLT PASTA SALAD

Once you try this pasta salad you will wonder why you've never eaten it before!

This can be kept in the fridge for up to 5 days once made, although I would recommend keeping the lettuce separately to avoid it browning.

You will have all the delicious flavours of a BLT sandwich, without the bread!

FAKE STEAK BAKES

PREP TIME
10 minutes

COOK TIME
20 minutes

READY IN
30 minutes

SERVINGS
6 bakes

CALORIES
239 Kcal serving

SOURCE
Sugar Pink Food

Ingredients

1 pack Kingsmill wholemeal thins
salt and black pepper
a large handful of chopped
mushrooms
4 stewing steaks, all fat removed
1 green pepper, 1 yellow pepper
1 carrot, sliced
1 large red onion
1tbsp Balsamic vinegar
1tbsp Worcestershire sauce
2 potatoes, diced
low calorie cooking spray
pinch of cayenne pepper
1tsp smoked paprika
200ml beef stock
4tbsp passata
1 egg, beaten

Steps

Place all the ingredients (except the thins!)
in a slow cooker, cook on low for 6 hours.

Alternatively cook in the oven for an hour
until filling is fully cooked.

Allow to cool slightly. Place mixture inside a
thin. Brush egg on each corner of thin and
press to seal.

Brush all over with egg and bake for 10-15
minutes on a medium heat.

Keep in the fridge for up to one week.

Notes
The filling can be bunged in the slow cooker all day, or in the oven.

TUNA MELT TOASTIE

PREP TIME
10 minutes

COOK TIME
10 minutes

READY IN
20 minutes

SERVINGS
1 toastie

CALORIES
373 Kcal toastie

SOURCE
Sugar Pink Food

Ingredients

2 slices 400g wholemeal bread

40g extra light cheddar cheese

½ tin tuna in brine

½ tin sweetcorn

1tbsp fat free fromage frais

a pinch salt and pepper

½tsp mustard powder

low calorie cooking spray

tin of beans or equivalent, to hold down the toastie in the pan

Steps

In a bowl, mix together the tuna, sweetcorn, fromage frais, mustard powder, salt and pepper. Spray 1 side of each slice of bread with the low calorie cooking spray, then turn them over. Grate the cheese. Add the tuna mix to one of the slices of bread, then top with the cheese.

Place the other slice of bread on top, cooking spray side up. Place the toastie in a heating frying pan, spray with more low calorie cooking spray if needed.

Use a spatula to press the toastie down, but not too hard to press the filling out. Cook for 2 minutes on one side, then use a spatula to flip it over.

Put a tin of beans on the cooked side of the toastie to press it down. This helps to melt the cheese. Flip again and cook until the bread is golden on each side and the cheese has melted.

Notes
One of my favourite pub lunches to have, but made at home with fewer calories.

CHICKEN & BACON SALAD

Chicken & Bacon Salad

Sugar Pink Food

PREP TIME
10 minutes

COOK TIME
20 minutes

READY IN
30 minutes

SERVINGS
2 people

CALORIES
313 Kcal serving

SOURCE
Sugar Pink Food

Ingredients

1 chicken breast per person

2 rashers of bacon

mixed salad of your choosing

1 slice 400g wholemeal bread

salt and pepper to taste

low calorie cooking spray

3tbsp fat free natural yoghurt

1 garlic clove, finely chopped

1tsp mixed Italian herbs

Steps

Preheat the oven to 200°C/400°F/gas 6.

Season the chicken breasts with salt and pepper, and place in the oven for 25-35 minutes.

To make the croutons, chop the bread into small squares and sprinkle with salt and pepper. Spray with low calorie spray and bake in the oven for 10-15 minutes or until golden brown and crunchy.

Mix the garlic clove with the yoghurt and mixed herbs and stir to make the dressing.

Lay the salad out on the plate and add the chicken, bacon and croutons. Add the dressing and enjoy.

Notes
A simple and tasty salad with home-baked, wholemeal croutons.

TORTILLA

PREP TIME
10 minutes

COOK TIME
30 minutes

READY IN
40 minutes

SERVINGS
4 servings

CALORIES
256 Kcal serving

SOURCE
Sugar Pink Food

Ingredients

3 medium potatoes, peeled and very thinly sliced
Low calorie cooking spray
6 large eggs, beaten
1 large onion, peeled and finely chopped
1 garlic clove, peeled and finely chopped
1 large green pepper and 1 large red pepper, halved, deseeded and finely chopped parsley

salt and black pepper

1 chicken breast, cooked and sliced
Mushrooms
Bacon

Steps

Place the sliced potatoes in a large saucepan and cover with water. Add a pinch of salt and bring to the boil. Cook for 3 minutes and then drain well.

Spray a frying pan with low calorie cooking spray and heat until hot. Add the potato slices, onions, peppers, bacon, garlic and fry until cooked. Add the cooked chicken

Season the eggs with salt and pepper and pour into the pan, packing the vegetables firmly together. Lower the heat and cook for 15-20 minutes until the base is set.

Place the tortilla under a preheated medium-hot grill and cook until golden and set.

Notes
This is a filling and tasty lunch and is great for lunch boxes. A tortilla is a Spanish omelette packed with vegetables and potatoes.

VEGETABLE SOUP

PREP TIME
10 minutes

COOK TIME
1 hour

READY IN
1 hour 10
minutes

SERVINGS
4 servings

CALORIES
157 Kcal serving

SOURCE
Sugar Pink Food

Ingredients

1 tin mixed bean salad
1 tin green lentils
2 tins chopped tomatoes
1 tin baked beans

a handful of split lentils
2 large leeks
1 large onion
4 large carrots
2 parsnips
green, red or yellow pepper
2 beef stock cube
salt and pepper
mixed herbs
stock (enough to cover all
ingredients)

Steps

Chop all vegetables and put everything in pan. Cover with stock and bring to the boil.

Simmer on a low heat until vegetables are soft, approximately 1 hour.

You can blend it or eat it chunky!

Notes

This recipe is packed with vegetables, so it is proven to speed up your weight loss. I wanted any help that I could get this week so made up a big batch of this

MIXED VEG COUS COUS

PREP TIME
10 minutes

COOK TIME
50 minutes

READY IN
1 hour

SERVINGS
4 servings

CALORIES
257 Kcal serving

SOURCE
Sugar Pink Food

Ingredients

150g couscous
1 clove garlic, finely chopped
4tbsp of diced red pepper
4 spring onions, sliced
1 red onion, finely sliced
150g cherry tomatoes
1 pinch of salt
1 pinch of ground black pepper
1 dash of balsamic vinegar
1tbsp of smoked paprika
1 courgette, chopped
1 red pepper finely chopped
Frylight
1 lime

Steps

Preheat the oven to 200°C.

Spray a baking tray with low calorie cooking spray. Place all the vegetables, including garlic cloves, into the dish.

Sprinkle with smoked paprika, balsamic vinegar and the juice of half a lime.

Roast vegetables until tender for approximately 45 minutes. Stir halfway through the cooking time.

If you are cooking this to serve immediately, then the best way to cook the couscous is to stir fry. If, like me, you are making up a batch for lunches, you can microwave the couscous in a heatproof bowl, covered with cling film, for 3 minutes on high. This can be done at the point of eating and mixed in with the ready cooked vegetables.

Squeeze the rest of the lime juice over the finished dish.

Notes

A delicious vegetarian couscous that is perfect for taking to work!

CRUSTLESS QUICHE

PREP TIME
10 minutes

COOK TIME
30 minutes

READY IN
40 minutes

SERVINGS
4 servings

CALORIES
229 Kcal serving

SOURCE
Sugar Pink Food

Ingredients

1 small onion, finely finely diced

4 cherry tomatoes, sliced

a handful of sweet corn

a handful of frozen peas

6 mushrooms, sliced

1 red pepper

6 eggs

bacon with fat removed

salt and pepper to taste

low fat cooking spray

2 cloves of garlic

2tbsp fat free fromage frais

Steps

Preheat the oven to 190°C.

Spray some low fat cooking spray into a frying pan

Add the bacon, onions, peppers and mushrooms and fry-off.

Add the rest of the vegetables and fry for 2 minutes.

In a measuring jug, whisk together eggs, garlic, chilli flakes, salt, pepper and fromage frais .

Spray some cooking oil around your quiche/pie dish and add the vegetables.

Add the egg mixture and mix everything around to make it even.

Put in the oven for 25 minutes or until the egg is baked, firm and golden, then enjoy.

Notes

A delicious crustless quiche recipe. You can add as many extra vegetables or flavours as you like.

POTATO & LEEK SOUP

PREP TIME
10 minutes

COOK TIME
40 minutes

READY IN
50 minutes

SERVINGS
4 servings

CALORIES
226 Kcal serving

SOURCE
Sugar Pink Food

Ingredients

6 large potatoes, chopped

1 onion, diced

3 garlic cloves, whole

1 leek, finely chopped

salt and pepper to taste

1 tbsp of horseradish sauce

1l of chicken stock

Steps

Place the potatoes, onion, garlic, leek and stock in a large saucepan.

Leave to simmer for around 30 minutes on a low heat or until all the vegetables are cooked and soft.

Add the horseradish and stir through and mix in well.

I put half the mixture in the blender at a time and blitz until completely smooth, but you can blend to any consistency you like! Add the salt and pepper to taste.

Notes
Traditional recipes are made with double cream, but mine is equally as creamy without it. I like my soups to be super smooth.

WELSH RAREBIT

PREP TIME
10 minutes

COOK TIME
10 minutes

READY IN
20 minutes

SERVINGS
4 servings

CALORIES
289 Kcal serving

SOURCE
Sugar Pink Food

Ingredients

4 slices wholemeal bread (from a small 400g loaf)

2 large eggs, separated

1tsp English mustard powder

1tsp mild paprika or cayenne pepper

160g reduced-fat cheddar cheese, finely grated

Steps

Preheat your grill to medium-high. Very lightly toast the slices of bread on both sides and place them on a baking tray.

Whisk the egg whites in a bowl until they form soft peaks and set aside. In a separate bowl, mix together the egg yolks, mustard powder, paprika or cayenne pepper and cheese. Fold in the egg whites and stir until well mixed.

Carefully spoon the mixture onto the slices of bread, place under the grill and cook for 3-4 minutes, or until puffed and golden brown

Notes

A delicious crustless quiche recipe. You can add as many extra vegetables or flavours as you like.

CHEESE TOASTIE & TOMATO SOUP

PREP TIME
10 minutes

COOK TIME
20 minutes

READY IN
30 minutes

SERVINGS
2 servings

CALORIES
437 Kcal

SOURCE
Sugar Pink Food

Ingredients

For the soup:

2 tins of chopped tomatoes

1 tin of baked beans

4 small pickled onions (or one large one), chopped in half

½ pint vegetable stock

a pinch of salt and pepper

1tsp Worcestershire sauce

½tsp sweetener

For the toasties:

2 slices 400g wholemeal bread

40g extra light cheddar cheese

Steps

Put all soup ingredients in a large saucepan and bring to the boil. As soon as the soup boils, reduce the heat to the lowest and allow to simmer.

Cover and leave for 15 minutes to simmer gently. Once cooled slightly, add to a blender and blitz until the mixture is completely smooth. Add some cheese on top and allow to melt.

Spray 1 side of each slice of bread with the low calorie cooking spray, then turn them over. Grate the cheese Add 40g extra light cheese to one of the slices of bread.

Place the other slice of bread on top, cooking spray side up.

Place the toastie in a heating frying pan, spray with more low calorie cooking spray if needed. Use a spatula to press the toastie down, but not too hard to press the filling out. You can also use a tin or something to keep them pressed down while cooking.

Notes

Cheese toasties are one of my favourite things on the planet, and I would eat them at every meal if I could!

GREEK PASTA SALAD

PREP TIME
15 minutes

COOK TIME
5 minutes

READY IN
20 minutes

SERVINGS
4 servings

CALORIES
389 Kcal

SOURCE
Sugar Pink Food

Ingredients

1tbsp olive oil

tbsp wholegrain mustard

250g cooked and cooled pasta of your choice

2tbsp balsamic vinegar

salt and freshly ground black pepper

180g feta cheese

½ cucumber, cubed

a handful of cherry tomatoes, sliced

8 olives, sliced up

½ red onion, finely diced

Steps

Whisk together the olive oil, mustard and balsamic vinegar, salt and pepper to make your dressing.

In a bowl, add the pasta, cucumber, feta, tomatoes and red onion.

Pour over the dressing, mix well and serve.

Leave in the fridge and consume within 3 days. Keep them pressed down while cooking.

Notes
This is a super easy to make Greek style pasta salad. It has lots of traditional Greek flavours. Once made it can be kept in the fridge for 3 days.

DINNER RECIPES

CREAMY BEEF STROGANOFF

PREP TIME
10 minutes

COOK TIME
20 minutes

READY IN
30 minutes

SERVINGS
4 portions

CALORIES
329 Kcal portion

SOURCE
Sugar Pink Food

Ingredients

beef or steak thinly sliced

1 onion finely diced

250g button mushrooms thinly sliced

2tsp Worcestershire sauce

1tsp white wine vinegar

1tsp mustard powder

500ml beef stock made up from cubes

200g Philadelphia lightest

sea salt and freshly ground black pepper

low calorie cooking spray

Steps

Spray a large frying pan with Low Calorie Cooking Spray and place on a medium heat. Add the beef, salt and pepper, and sear in the pan.

Remove the meat from the pan, and add the white wine vinegar and Worcestershire shire sauce. Add the onions and mushrooms and cook.

Add the mustard powder, stir and leave to simmer.

Add the stock to the pan and reduce for 15 minutes.

Stir in the Philadelphia over a low heat, making sure there are no lumps of cheese remaining.

Add the beef back into the pan and stir well. I like to serve mine with rice.

Notes

This is my twist on a tasty classic beef stroganoff with steak and mushrooms. This is so simple to make and tasty to eat, and amazingly, is also lower in calories.

CREAMY BEEF STROGANOFF

I have been paying special attention to creating tasty dishes that are suitable to make on a busy weeknight evening, and are easy to throw everything together. This dish takes a maximum of 30 minutes to prepare and cook.

The key to making low-calorie meals is to swap usually fatty meats for lower fat content or even removing the fat from the meat.

If you buy beef chunks for this recipe and they come with fat, just remove it with scissors before cooking.

ROAST DINNER TRAYBAKE

PREP TIME
10 minutes

COOK TIME
1 hour

READY IN
1 hour 10
minutes

SERVINGS
4 servings

CALORIES
219 Kcal serving

SOURCE
Sugar Pink Food

Ingredients

2 large chicken breasts, skinless
a handful of chopped carrots
a handful of chopped broccoli
a handful of green beans, chopped
1 red onion, chopped
a handful of chopped cauliflower
a handful of Jersey Royal potatoes,
chopped
a pinch of salt and pepper
a pinch of smoked paprika
a pinch of mixed herbs
1 oxo cube
100ml red wine to go in the
bottom of the tray
Optional to serve: Yorkshire pudding
and pigs in blankets (not included in
calories)

Steps

Preheat the oven to 170°C.

Add your vegetables to the tray.

Top with the chicken breasts, then
season with salt, pepper and mixed
herbs.

Add the red wine to the vegetables in
the bottom of the tray.

Cook for 1 hour, or until the vegetables
have softened and the chicken is cooked
through.

Use the red wine, vegetables and meat
juices mixed with 1 oxo cube to make
the gravy. Add 1tsp of gravy granules if
needed to thicken, and add the calories.

Notes

I love a good roast dinner, but sometimes cooking a roast requires a whole lot of
effort! One weekend I really fancied a roast dinner, but definitely did not fancy
having to make one. So I came up with this alternative.

SLOW COOKER BEEF CASSEROLE

PREP TIME
10 minutes

COOK TIME
3 hours

READY IN
3 hours 10
minutes

SERVINGS
4 servings

CALORIES
584 Kcal serving

SOURCE
Sugar Pink Food

Ingredients

750g lean stewing beef, all visible
fat removed, diced
1 large red onion, roughly chopped
low calorie cooking spray
2 garlic cloves, crushed
600ml beef stock (gan be made up
from cubes)
1tbsp tomato purée
1tbsp Worcestershire sauce
200g carrots, chopped
100g mushrooms, chopped
200g Jersey Royal potatoes, chopped
a handful of frozen peas
1tsp dried parsley
1tsp smoked paprika
Dumplings:
100g self-raising flour
a pinch of salt and black pepper
1 egg yolk, lightly beaten
1tsp olive oil

Steps

Add all the casserole ingredients into
your slow cooker and mix well.

Cook on low for 7 hours, or high for 3
hours. If you don't have a slow cooker,
cook in the oven at 160°C for 2 hours.

To make the dumplings, add the flour to
a mixing bowl with the salt and pepper.
Add the egg and oil and mix, adding just
enough cold water to bring it together
as a dough (about 4tbsp). Separate out
into 8 dumplings.

Be careful not to add too much water as
this will ruin the dumplings and they
will turn to mush!

Add the dumplings in the last 20
minutes of cooking.

Notes
Because you can't beat a classic casserole! This one comes with these tasty, lower
in calorie dumplings.

PHILLY CHEESESTEAK PASTA

I first created and posted my slimming friendly Philly Cheesesteak Fries recipe way back in 2015, and it is still one of my most popular recipes to this day. This is a pasta dish with all the Philly Cheesesteak flavours.

Here is how the dish looked before I added the cheese on top! You could easily make this dish with beef steaks as well as beef mince.

If you are going to use steak slices, then add these at the very end of cooking.

PHILLY CHEESESTEAK PASTA

PREP TIME
10 minutes

COOK TIME
30 minutes

READY IN
40 minutes

SERVINGS
4 servings

CALORIES
476 Kcal serving

SOURCE
Sugar Pink Food

Ingredients

500g 5% fat beef mince
low calorie cooking spray
salt and black pepper
a large handful of mushrooms
1 green pepper
1 yellow pepper
1 large red onion
1tbsp balsamic vinegar
1tbsp Worcestershire sauce
pinch of cayenne pepper
1tsp smoked paprika
160g extra light cheddar
250g dried pasta
1 tub extra light cream cheese
1 garlic clove, crushed
100ml beef stock (made up from a cube)

Steps

Preheat the oven to 180°C. Boil the pasta as per pack instructions. Spray a frying pan with low calorie cooking spray, and add in the peppers, onions and garlic. Cook for around 3 minutes, or until the vegetables have softened.

Add in the beef mince, balsamic vinegar, Worcestershire sauce, cayenne pepper and smoked paprika. Season with salt and pepper, and cook until the beef is no longer pink. Turn the heat right down. Mix in the cream cheese until melted, careful not to let it overheat. Sometimes you can do this without the hob heat being on. Add the beef stock and mix. Add half of the cheddar cheese, mix until melted. Add the pasta and mix well.

Top with grated cheddar and pop in the oven to melt. If you don't have an oven proof pan, transfer mixture to a large greased baking dish and then top with cheese. Bake for 10-25 minutes or until the cheese has completely melted.

Notes
I first created and posted my slimming friendly Philly Cheesesteak Fries recipe way back in 2015, and it is still one of my most popular recipes to this day. This is a pasta based twist!

CHICKEN & BACON DIRTY RICE

PREP TIME
10 minutes

COOK TIME
20 minutes

READY IN
30 minutes

SERVINGS
4 servings

CALORIES
370 Kcal serving

SOURCE
Sugar Pink Food

Ingredients

200g rice long grain rice, cooked
500g diced skinless chicken breast
4 bacon medallions, all visible fat
removed, cut into strips
1 red pepper sliced
1 red onion diced
2 spring onions, finely chopped
1 tin of sweetcorn, drained
2tsp smoked paprika
1tbsp Cajun seasoning
1tsp minced garlic
1 chicken stock cube, dissolved in
125ml water
2tbsp Worcestershire sauce
1tsp balsamic vinegar
low calorie cooking spray

Steps

Spray a large frying pan with low
calorie cooking spray, then fry the
onions, bacon and chicken until they
are browned.

Add the smoked paprika, garlic,
Worcestershire sauce, Cajun seasoning
and balsamic vinegar. Stir and allow to
cook for another minute

Add the peppers, spring onion,
sweetcorn and stock. Cook for a further
2 minutes.

Stir in the cooked rice, mixing well to
ensure it is fully coated in the flavours.

Notes

For a long time now I have wanted to have a go at making 'Dirty Rice'. This is a
traditional Cajun and Creole dish made from white rice which gets a "dirty"
colour from being cooked with the flavours and meat.

SPINACH & FETA FILO PARCELS

PREP TIME
10 minutes

COOK TIME
20 minutes

READY IN
30 minutes

SERVINGS
4 parcels

CALORIES
136 Kcal parcel

SOURCE
Sugar Pink Food

Ingredients

1 small onion, finely chopped

1 garlic cloves, crushed

low calorie cooking spray

I bag of Spinach, stalks trimmed and chopped

75g feta, crumbled into small pieces

juice of 1 lemon

filo pastry 2 sheets

Steps

Heat the oven to 180°C/fan 160°C/gas 4.

In a saucepan sprayed with low calorie cooking spray, fry the onion and garlic until soft but not browned.

Add the spinach and stir until it wilts and any liquid dries off (it will look like lots of spinach, but it shrinks a lot!)

Add the mixture to a bowl, then add the feta cheese and lemon juice. Spray a sheet of filo and cut it length ways into 3 strips.

Put 2tbsp of the mix at the top of each strip and fold each diagonally to make a small triangle, then continue to fold over down the length of the pastry. Repeat with the remaining filling and pastry.

Arrange the parcels on a baking sheet and spray them with more cooking spray. Bake for 18-20 minutes, or until they're golden brown and cooked through.

Notes

This recipe is vegetarian, super delicious, easy to make and low calorie. I guess you could describe them as little British samosas.

GARLIC CHICKEN & PROSCIUTTO PASTA

PREP TIME
10 minutes

COOK TIME
30 minutes

READY IN
40 minutes

SERVINGS
4 servings

CALORIES
520 Kcal serving

SOURCE
Sugar Pink Food

Ingredients

400g diced skinless chicken breast
1tsp Italian herbs
1 garlic clove, minced
3 slices of prosciutto ham, in small slices
1 red pepper, sliced
1 onion finely diced
1 carton of passata
a pinch of salt and pepper
400g dried pasta
120g extra light cheddar cheese

Steps

Preheat the oven to gas mark 6, 200°C, fan 180°C. Spray a frying pan with low calorie cooking spray. Add the onions and peppers and stir fry, then removed and set aside when cooked.

Turn the heat to medium. Sprinkle the diced chicken with the Italian herbs and garlic. Fry-off and seal. Meanwhile, parboil the pasta as per packet instructions.

Add the passata, salt, and pepper to the chicken in the pan, and turn off the heat. Then add the slices of prosciutto.

Drain the cooked pasta and pour into a large oven proof dish. Top with the passata, chicken and mix. Stir until everything is mixed well. Top with cheese, then bake for 20 minutes, or until cheese is bubbling.

Notes

This is what I call a perfect 'weeknight' recipe. It is really easy to throw together on a post-work evening, and is so tasty that the whole family will enjoy it!
If you really like garlic, you can add as many cloves as you like to this recipe.

GARLIC CHICKEN & PROSCIUTTO PASTA

This is what I call a perfect 'weeknight' recipe. It is really easy to throw together on a post-work evening, and is so tasty that the whole family will enjoy it!

If you really like garlic, you can add as many cloves as you like to this recipe. I mean, does anyone even follow the amount of garlic I say anyway?

You could use any type of pasta for this, but I love the twists.

THAI CHICKEN STRIPS

PREP TIME
10 minutes

COOK TIME
20 minutes

READY IN
30 minutes

SERVINGS
4 servings

CALORIES
385 Kcal serving

SOURCE
Sugar Pink Food

Ingredients

2 shallots, peeled

2 large garlic cloves

a few fresh coriander leaves

½tsp lazy ginger

½tsp lemongrass (I used this)

1 red chilli, finely chopped

juice and zest of 2 limes

1tbsp of fat free natural Greek yogurt

2 skinless chicken breasts cut into strips, or some chicken mini fillets

Steps

Add the shallots, garlic, coriander, ginger, lemongrass, chilli, lime juice, zest and yogurt to a blender. Blitz to form a smooth paste.

Add the chicken strips to the paste mix, and move around to get an even coating.

Spray a frying pan with low calorie cooking spray, then add the strips to the heated pan.

Cook for around 6 minutes on each side, depending on the thickness of the strips, or until the chicken is fully cooked through. Always check before serving.

(See page133 for coconut and lime rice)

Notes
This is my take on some Thai Green Chicken Strips, which goes perfectly with some coconut and lime rice.

SWEET CHILLI CHICKEN BREASTS

PREP TIME
2 hours
(marinade time)

COOK TIME
25 minutes

READY IN
2 hours 25
minutes

SERVINGS
4 servings

CALORIES
430 Kcal serving

SOURCE
Sugar Pink Food

Ingredients

2 large skinless chicken breasts

1 whole red chilli finely chopped

80ml white wine vinegar

1tsp sea salt

1 clove garlic grated

1tsp tomato purée

½tsp honey

1tbsp granulated sweetener

low calorie cooking spray

Steps

To make the sauce, spray a pan with low calorie cooking spray and fry-off the garlic and chilli.

Add the white wine vinegar, salt, sweetener and tomato purée, stir well. Bring to the boil and then reduce the heat. Add the honey and stir well, until the sauce starts to reduce. Allow to cool. Any leftover sauce can be kept in a jar as a dipping sauce.

Once cooled, pour the sauce over the chicken breasts, and leave to marinate in the fridge for 2 hours.

When ready to cook, place the chicken breasts on an oven proof tray, and pour over the remaining sweet chilli. Cook at 200 degrees for 25 minutes, or until the chicken is cooked through.

Notes
This is a tasty sweet chilli chicken breast that is easy to make, and lower in calories.

SWEET CHILLI CHICKEN BREASTS

This is a tasty dish that serves 2, and is sweet chilli chicken breasts with a cream garlic mashed potato. I think I have a method to get the creamiest mashed potato, without having to add in any butter or fat *(see page 129 for the recipe)*.

I serve my meal with salad and vegetables, but you can add any kind of healthy vegetables or salad you like! It is always best to fill your plate up with as many healthy vegetables as possible.

TOAD IN THE HOLE

PREP TIME
20 minutes

COOK TIME
1 hour

READY IN
1 hour 20
minutes

SERVINGS
4 servings

CALORIES
349 Kcal serving

SOURCE
Sugar Pink Food

Ingredients

The batter works best if left for a few hours in the fridge, or better still overnight.

4 low fat sausages (adjust calorie count accordingly)

30g plain flour

2 eggs

75ml skimmed milk

Frylight

a pinch of salt and pepper

Steps

In a bowl, whisk together the eggs, flour, milk and salt until smooth. Cover and place in the fridge at least overnight.

When ready to cook the meal, preheat the oven to 190°C.

Put the sausages in the dish you are going to use to cook the toad in the hole, place in the oven for 10 minutes, until they are slightly browned.

Remove and spray a generous amount of Frylight on the dish. Pour over the Yorkshire pudding mix and cook for 20 minutes, keep an eye on it but do not open the oven door for the first 10 minutes, as you could lose all the puff!

When the Yorkshire pudding is golden and risen, remove and serve.

Notes

This batter mix recipe really does work best when left overnight, as it helps it to rise properly. It goes really well with low fat sausages.

SUGAR PINK FOOD RECIPES

BBQ BEEF BRISKET

PREP TIME
10 minutes

COOK TIME
4 hours

READY IN
4 hours 10

SERVINGS
4 servings

CALORIES
485 Kcal serving

SOURCE
Sugar Pink Food

Ingredients

1½tbsp yellow mustard seeds
1tbsp black peppercorns
2tbsp coriander seeds
2tbsp cumin seeds
1 sweetner
1tbsp smoked paprika
1tsp cayenne pepper
2kg whole piece of brisket beef
400ml beef stock
BBQ Sauce
5tbsp Worcestershire sauce
1tsp mustard powder
500g passata
3tbsp balsamic vinegar
2 cloves of garlic, crushed
3 tbsp sweetener
salt and freshly ground black pepper
1tsp smoked paprika
¼ pint coke zero
beef juices

Steps

For the brisket, put the coriander seeds, cumin seeds, mustard seeds and peppercorns in a frying pan and toast over a medium heat for a few minutes, do not burn. Allow to cool.

Once cooled, add the spices to a pestle and mortar and crush to a powder. Add the sweetener, smoked paprika and cayenne pepper, and mix together. Score the beef and rub the spice mix all over the joint. Roll the joint up and tie securely in several places using kitchen string. Cover with cling film and place in the fridge overnight.

The next day, preheat the oven to 160°C/325°F/Gas 3. Place the brisket on a wire rack inside a roasting tray and pour the beef stock around the outside. Cover the whole tray with aluminium foil to prevent any moisture escaping. Place in the oven to cook slowly for 4-6 hours, or slow cooker. Add some water if it looks low or dey. Remove from the oven.

Add all the BBQ sauce ingredients to a pan, bring to the boil then reduce to simmer. Meanwhile, remove the brisket from the rack and pull the meat apart using a fork. Add the shredded brisket to the simmering sauce along with any juices left in the roasting tray. Bring back to a very low simmer and cook for a further 10-15 minutes or until mixed and coated.

Notes

Brisket is a cut of meat from the breast or lower chest of beef. It can sometimes be quite tough, but when cooked properly it is absolutely beautiful.

SUGAR PINK FOOD RECIPES

BBQ BEEF BRISKET

Brisket is a cut of meat from the breast or lower chest of beef. It can sometimes be quite tough, but when cooked properly it is absolutely beautiful.

My favourite way to cook it is with lashings of sugar free BBQ sauce in the slow cooker. When it's ready it falls apart and shreds to create this gorgeous meaty treat.

Creating a rub for the meat and marinating overnight helps take this dish to the next level. There is plenty of flavour and a rich smoky BBQ taste.

You can enjoy this without any of the guilt!! I recommend serving it with some fat free coleslaw, cheese and fries.

HUNTERS CHICKEN

PREP TIME
10 minutes

COOK TIME
35 minutes

READY IN
45 minutes

SERVINGS
4 servings

CALORIES
404 Kcal serving

SOURCE
Sugar Pink Food

Ingredients

2 large chicken breasts

4 rashers of bacon- all visible fat removed

80g extra light cheddar cheese

5tbsp Worcestershire sauce

1tsp mustard powder

500g passata

3tbsp balsamic vinegar

2 cloves of garlic, crushed

3tbsp sweetener

salt and freshly ground black pepper

1tsp smoked paprika

¼ pint Coca-Cola zero

1 beef stock cube

Steps

Preheat the oven to 180°C.

In a small bowl mix passata, Worcestershire sauce, balsamic vinegar, mustard powder, garlic, smoked paprika, sweetener, seasoning, Coca-Cola and stock cube. Mix well to form your BBQ sauce.

Wrap the chicken breasts in the bacon, then place in an oven proof dish. Cook in the oven for 10 minutes.

Remove and then cover the chicken in the BBQ sauce and top each breast with 40g extra light cheese.

Bake for 25 minutes, ensuring the chicken is cooked through before serving.

Notes
My BBQ Chicken Stack recipe has been one of the most popular recipes on my site, and one of the oldest. This is my new and improved recipe, with my best ever BBQ sauce.

LOADED CHICKEN BURGER

PREP TIME
15 minutes

COOK TIME
30 minutes

READY IN
45 minutes

SERVINGS
2 burgers

CALORIES
542 Kcal serving

SOURCE
Sugar Pink Food

Ingredients

2 small skinless chicken breast
2 slices of 400g wholemeal bread
1tsp oregano
1½tsp chilli powder (adjust to your spice taste)
1tsp ground sage
1tsp basil
1tsp pepper
2tsp salt
2tsp paprika
1tsp garlic powder
1tsp garlic salt

1 egg
To serve:
Lettuce
1tsp extra light mayo
2 Schär gluten free white ciabatta rolls
2 American reduced fat cheese slices

Steps

Blitz the bread in a food processor until it's created fine breadcrumbs. Put into a bowl and add all of the seasonings and mix until everything is blended together to create your coating.

Crack the egg into a dish and whisk. The chicken needs to be dipped in the egg and then to the breadcrumb mixture, and repeated to get an even coating. Tip: Only use one hand for touching the egg and the other hand for touching the breadcrumbs. This stops a sticky mixture on your fingers!

Bake the chicken in the oven for 20-25 minutes on a medium heat. Always check the chicken is cooked all the way through before serving.

Mix the salsa ingredients together.

To serve, add ½tsp of extra light mayo on the base of a warmed Schär gluten free white ciabatta roll, then put lettuce on top of that.

Notes

A tasty Southern Fried Chicken style burger! Perfect for any Fakeaway evening in!

SLOW COOKER MEATBALLS

PREP TIME
10 minutes

COOK TIME
3 hours

READY IN
3 hours 10 minutes

SERVINGS
4 servings

CALORIES
277 Kcal serving

SOURCE
Sugar Pink Food

Ingredients

500g 5% lean beef mince
2 bacon medallions, all fat removed, sliced into strips
1 red pepper, finely chopped
1 onion, finely chopped
1tsp Italian herbs
2 cloves of garlic, crushed
a pinch of salt and black pepper
500g of passata
1 beef oxo cube, crumbled
1tbsp of balsamic vinegar
2tbsp of Worcestershire sauce
1tbsp tomato purée

Steps

In a large bowl mix the mince, half the minced garlic, salt and pepper.

Using your hands, mix together well and roll into 12 even meatballs.

Spray a frying pan with low calorie cooking spray and fry-off the meatballs until they are browned on the outside and sealed.

Add the meatballs with the rest of the ingredients to the slow cooker and leave for 3 hours on high or 6 hours on low.

Notes

This recipe requires a little bit of effort before hand making the meatballs, but is totally worth it. You could of course use pre-made low fat meatballs instead to save even more time.

SLOW COOKER MEATBALLS

Slow cooking is a real comfort to me, there's nothing better than walking in to the smell of a cooked dinner when you get in from work.

This recipe requires a little bit of effort before hand making the meatballs, but is totally worth it. You could of course use pre-made low fat meatballs instead to save even more time.

Apart from browning off the meatballs, this recipe is pretty much dump and go. You can chop the onions and peppers as precisely or as roughly as you want.

CREAMY PESTO PASTA

PREP TIME
5 minutes

COOK TIME
15 hours

READY IN
20 minutes

SERVINGS
4 servings

CALORIES
191 Kcal serving

SOURCE
Sugar Pink Food

Ingredients

200g dried pasta

250g tub of Quark

a large handful of fresh basil

a handful of fresh parsley

3 garlic cloves, peeled and whole

juice of 1 lemon

a large pinch of salt and pepper

2tbsp of the water the pasta was
cooked in

Steps

Boil the pasta as per the pack
instructions.

Add the rest of the ingredients into a
blender, and blitz until the sauce is
smooth.

Drain the cooked pasta, but keep some
of the water aside, then add the pasta
back into the empty pan.

Stir the pesto sauce through the cooked
pasta and serve. Add some pasta water
to make it smoother.

Notes
Is there any better comfort food than a big bowl of pasta? Even better when it's a
big plate of creamy pesto pasta! Pesto is traditionally made with blended pine
nuts, parmesan and oil, so isn't the healthiest of meals.

SAUSAGE & VEGETABLE BAKE

PREP TIME
10 minutes

COOK TIME
3 hours

READY IN
3 hours 10
minutes

SERVINGS
4 servings

CALORIES
390 Kcal serving

SOURCE
Sugar Pink Food

Ingredients

10 chicken sausages
1 red pepper, sliced
1 yellow pepper, sliced
1 orange pepper, sliced
1 courgette sliced
1 red onion, sliced
sea salt and black pepper
550g passata
2 garlic cloves peeled and crushed
1 handful chopped basil
1tsp smoked paprika

For the crumb:
60g wholemeal roll per person
(HEb)
30g parmesan per person (HEa)

Steps

Preheat the oven to 180°C/160°C fan/gas mark 5.

In a large roasting tray place all vegetables. Spray with low calorie cooking spray, salt and pepper. Cook in the oven for 15-20 minutes.

At the same time cook the sausages in the oven for 12-14 minutes.

Whilst they cook, add garlic into a small saucepan, spray with low calorie cooking spray and fry on a medium heat for 2 minutes. Add the passata and simmer for a further 10-15 minutes. Season to taste and stir in the chopped basil. For the crumb topping add the wholemeal rolls and parmesan to a blender and blitz until crumbed.

Once everything is cooked, take a deep baking dish and put the sausages, vegetables and tomato sauce in, then top with the crumb

Put the whole dish back into the oven for 20-25 minutes and enjoy with a crisp green salad. Enjoy!

Notes
Bursting with peppery watercress and lemon freshness, these zesty chicken sausages go amazingly well in this Mediterranean vegetable bake with cheese crumb.

CHICKEN FRIED RICE

PREP TIME
10 minutes

COOK TIME
10 hours

READY IN
20 minutes

SERVINGS
4 servings

CALORIES
390 Kcal serving

SOURCE
Sugar Pink Food

Ingredients

500g diced chicken breasts

200g long-grain rice (uncooked weight), cooked and left to go cold

200g peas

a handful of mushrooms finely sliced

½ onion finely diced

1tbsp soy sauce

1 clove of garlic, finely chopped

a pinch of salt

Frylight

1 egg

Steps

Add the garlic and diced chicken breast to a frying pan over a medium heat.

Spray with Frylight.

Then add the peas, onions and mushrooms.

Fry-off for 3 minutes.

Finally add the rice, soy sauce, salt and pepper. Spray with Frylight and fry for 5 minutes. If the rice is looking pale add some more soy sauce.

Crack the egg into one side of the pan, then stir through the rice until cooked.

Notes

A super simple and tasty Chicken Fried Rice recipe that's perfect for any Fakeaway Feast!

SLOW COOKER GREEK CHICKEN

PREP TIME
10 minutes

COOK TIME
4 hours

READY IN
4 hours 10
minutes

SERVINGS
4 servings

CALORIES
390 Kcal serving

SOURCE
Sugar Pink Food

Ingredients

2 large chicken breasts

juice of 1 lemon

3 garlic cloves, finely crushed

2tsp of red wine vinegar

2tbsp of Greek yogurt

2tsp of dried oregano

2-4tsp of Greek seasoning (or 1tsp
sage, salt and pepper)

½ a small red onion
Tzatziki:

2 large tbsp of fat free Greek Yogurt

1 small cucumber, chopped into
small cubes

pinch of salt and pepper

Steps

Add all the chicken mix ingredients into
the slow cooker.

Cook on low for 6 hours or high for 4
hours. Once the chicken is cooked,
shred the chicken and return to the pot.

Mix all the ingredients together for the
Tzatziki.

Pile the chicken and vegetables high on
your pita bread, top with Tzatziki and
enjoy!

Notes

I absolutely love Greek food, especially a gyros. A gyro or gyros is a Greek dish
made from meat cooked on a vertical rotisserie, kind of like a Greek kebab.

PIZZA TOPPED FRIES

PREP TIME
10 minutes

COOK TIME
40 minutes

READY IN
50 minutes

SERVINGS
4 servings

CALORIES
347 Kcal serving

SOURCE
Sugar Pink Food

Ingredients

4 cloves garlic, peeled and finely sliced
1 bunch fresh basil, leaves picked and torn
3 x 400g good-quality tinned plum tomatoes
Sea salt
1tsp smoked paprika
Freshly ground black pepper
Mozzarella
6 slices of pepperoni (or other toppings of choice)
900g medium sized Maris Piper potatoes
low calorie cooking spray

Steps

Preheat the oven to 240°C, Peel the potatoes. Slice lengthwise into rectangular chips. Bring a large saucepan of salted water to the boil. Add the chips and cook for 4 minutes. Drain and leave aside for 10 minutes to dry.

Place in an ovenproof dish and spray with Frylight, salt and pepper and bake in the oven for 30 minutes. While the chips are cooking, prepare the sauce. To make the pizza sauce add garlic to a frying pan and colour slightly. Add the basil and tomatoes and bring to the boil. Using the back of a wooden spoon, mush and squash the tomatoes as much as you can.

Season the sauce with salt and pepper. As soon as it comes to the boil, remove the pan from the heat.

Top the chips with pizza sauce, then top with cheese and any other toppings. Place in the oven and bake until cheese is melted and golden

Notes
Because what could be better than pizza toppings on chips?

MEXICAN ENCHILADA LASAGNE

PREP TIME
10 minutes

COOK TIME
45 minutes

READY IN
55 minutes

SERVINGS
4 servings

CALORIES
521 Kcal serving

SOURCE
Sugar Pink Food

Ingredients

4 chicken breasts
salt and pepper
2tsp cumin powder
2tsp garlic powder
1tsp smoked paprika
2 cartons passata
2 cloves garlic, minced
1 whole green seeded and finely
chopped (leave out if you don't want
spice!)
1tsp sweetener
1 large red pepper, chopped
1 red onion, finely diced
For the lasagne:
1 pack dried lasagne sheets
160g extra light cheddar (remember to
allow 40g per serving as a healthy extra)
1 tub fat free cottage cheese mixed with
1tsp smoked paprika

Steps

To make the filling, put all the ingredients apart from the pasta and cheese in the slow cooker/large oven dish and cook on low for 7 hours in the slow cooker or a preheated oven at 200°C/400°F/gas for 45 minutes, or until the chicken is cooked through.

Remove the chicken breasts from the pot and pull apart and shred with 2 forks. Split the passata, pepper and red onion sauce in half and set one half to the side. Mix the shredded chicken in with the other half of the sauce.
Place a layer of the chicken mixture then a layer of pasta sheets in an oven proof dish. Take a few spoonfuls of cottage cheese and spread over the lasagne sheets. Repeat until all the mixture is used.

Top with the rest of the passata and cheese, and bake in the oven for 30 minutes or until the pasta has cooked and the cheese is bubbling.

Notes
I love Mexican food and enchiladas are probably one of my favourite dishes. Once baked the texture is really similar to the real thing, so much so that you won't believe it's not a real enchilada!

SUGAR PINK FOOD RECIPES

MEXICAN ENCHILADA LASAGNE

This is a delicious twist on a lasagne, by adding a Mexican kick and succulent chicken.

This dish reminds me of all of the flavours of enchiladas, but without all the tortillas.

I like to serve this with a big side salad!

CREAMY TOMATO & CHICKEN PASTA

PREP TIME
10 minutes

COOK TIME
30 minutes

READY IN
40 minutes

SERVINGS
4 servings

CALORIES
436 Kcal serving

SOURCE
Sugar Pink Food

Ingredients

400g diced skinless chicken breast
6 bacon medallions, cubed up
1 red pepper, slice
1 onion finely diced
a handful of mushrooms, sliced
a handful of cherry tomatoes, halved
1 carton of passata
2tbsp quark
1 garlic clove, minced
a pinch of salt and pepper
1tsp Italian herbs
400g dried pasta
35g cheddar cheese per quarter

Steps

Preheat the oven to gas mark 6, 200°C, fan 180°C. Spray a frying pan with low calorie cooking spray.

Turn the heat to medium and add the chicken and fry-off to seal. Add the bacon and fry for 3 minutes. Meanwhile, boil the pasta as per packet instructions.

When the chicken and bacon has cooked, remove from the pan and set aside. Add vegetables to the frying pan and stir fry. Add the passata, garlic, salt, pepper and Italian herbs to the vegetables mix and stir well.

Add the chicken and bacon back into the pan and mix well. Pour the cooked pasta into a large oven proof dish. Top with the passata, chicken and bacon mix and stir until everything is mixed well.

Bake for 20 minutes, then remove and stir through the quark. Top with cheese then bake for a further 10 minutes, or until cheese is bubbling.

Notes

A delicious weeknight pasta meal that you can enjoy again and again!

SHREDDED BBQ CHICKEN

PREP TIME
10 minutes

COOK TIME
3 hours

READY IN
3 hours 10
minutes

SERVINGS
4 servings

CALORIES
191 Kcal serving

SOURCE
Sugar Pink Food

Ingredients

4 large chicken breasts
½l chicken stock
Salt and pepper
BBQ Sauce
5tbsp Worcestershire sauce
1tsp mustard powder
500g passata
3tbsp balsamic vinegar
2 cloves of garlic, crushed
3tbsp sweetener
1tsp smoked paprika

Steps

Place the chicken breasts in the slow cooker with the stock. Season with salt and pepper.

Cook for 4 hours on high or 8 hours on low.

Fry-off the garlic then add the rest of the BBQ sauce ingredients. Leave to simmer and reduce down.

Once cooked, remove the chicken from the slow cooker and place on a chopping board. Shred the chicken with 2 forks.

Split the chicken in half and mix one half with the BBQ sauce.

Allow to cool then refrigerate as soon as possible, limiting the amount of time it is exposed to room temperatures. Never leave the chicken at room temperature for more than 2hours. Cooked chicken can be stored for up to 3 or 4days in a refrigerator in a sealed container.

Notes

Cooking on weekday evenings can be tough after a long day at work. I am always trying to think of ways to make life easier for myself and this is a great meal you can prepare for the week ahead.

BBQ BURRITO BOWLS

PREP TIME
10 minutes

COOK TIME
20 minutes

READY IN
30 minutes

SERVINGS
4 servings

CALORIES
390 Kcal serving

SOURCE
Sugar Pink Food

Ingredients

1 pre-made BBQ shredded chicken
1 onion, diced
1 cup of uncooked extra-long grain rice
1 14.5 oz can of diced tomatoes, drained
1 tin of tacco beans
½ tsp garlic powder
½ tsp chili powder
1 tsp cumin
1 tsp smoked paprika
600ml chicken stock
80g low fat cheddar cheese (or 40g per potion)
salt and pepper
freshly diced tomatoes
low calorie cooking spray
1 red chilli, chopped

Steps

Fry-off the onions and chilli in a large frying pan. Spray with low calorie cooking spray to prevent sticking.

Once the onions have fried-off, add the uncooked rice and mix for about 2 minutes or until some grains start to turn brown.

Stir in the tacco beans, shredded chicken, tinned tomatoes, chicken stock, garlic powder, chili powder, smoked paprika and cumin.

Bring to a simmer, cover and reduce to a low heat. Cook for about 20 minutes or until rice is tender.

Sprinkle with cheese and chopped tomatoes, cover and set aside to allow the cheese to melt.

Notes

At the weekend I often cook a batch of shredded chicken to help make weekday meals easier. I used my BBQ chicken for this dish and it came out amazing!

SUGAR PINK FOOD RECIPES

CHICKEN PARMIGIANA

PREP TIME
10 minutes

COOK TIME
35 minutes

READY IN
45 minutes

Sugar Pink Food

SERVINGS
4 servings

CALORIES
390 Kcal serving

SOURCE
Sugar Pink Food

Ingredients

2 large, skinless chicken breasts, halved through the middle

2 eggs, beaten

120g wholemeal breadcrumbs

25g parmesan, grated

2 garlic cloves, crushed

1 carton passata

1tsp sweetener sugar

1tsp dried oregano

half a 125g ball of light mozzarella

low calorie cooking spray

1 beef tomato, sliced

Steps

Place the chicken breasts between cling film sheets and bash out with a rolling pin until they are the thickness of a £1 coin. Dip in the egg, then breadcrumbs, mixed with the grated parmesan. Set aside on a plate in the fridge while you make the sauce.

Spray the low calorie cooking spray and fry-off the garlic for 1 minute, then tip in passata, sugar and oregano. Season and simmer for 5-10 minutes.

Heat grill to high and cook the chicken for 5 minutes each side, then remove. Pour the tomato sauce into a shallow ovenproof dish and top with the chicken. Top with the tomato slices. Scatter over the mozzarella and grill for 3-4 minutes until the cheese has melted and the sauce is bubbling.

Notes

Chicken Parmigiana is a chicken dish based on the Italian Parmigiana. It consists of breaded chicken breast, or chicken schnitzel, covered with a tomato-based Neapolitan sauce and cheese.

BEEF KOFTA KEBABS

PREP TIME
10 minutes

COOK TIME
25 minutes

READY IN
35 minutes

SERVINGS
4 servings

CALORIES
409 Kcal serving

SOURCE
Sugar Pink Food

Ingredients

400g extra lean beef mince

½ an onion, grated

2 garlic cloves, minced

1tsp dried parsley

1tsp smoked paprika

½tsp cumin

salt and pepper

½tsp cayenne pepper

kebab sticks

1tbsp fat free fromage frais

Steps

Heat oven to 200°C.

Combine all the kebab ingredients in a bowl and mix together well. Leave in the fridge for 1 hour.

Meanwhile, mix the rice, sweetcorn, peas, tomatoes and feta together and stuff into the halved sweet chillies

Once the meat has been in the fridge for the hour, gently pack small amounts of the meat mixture around the kebab skewers to make a 4-inch long sausage shape on each stick.

Notes
Tasty homemade beef kofta kebabs that are really easy to make, as well as being extra delicious!

STUFFED BACON & ONION BURGERS

PREP TIME
10 minutes

COOK TIME
3 hours

READY IN
3 hours 10
minutes

SERVINGS
4 servings

CALORIES
490Kcal

SOURCE
Sugar Pink Food

Ingredients

1 small onion, finely chopped
2tsp Worcestershire sauce
2 garlic cloves, crushed
Bacon, all fat removed
500g extra lean beef mince
1tbsp fat free fromage frais
5tbsp Worcestershire sauce (bbq sauce)
2tbsp Worcestershire sauce (burgers)
1tsp mustard powder
500g passata
3tbsp balsamic vinegar
3tbsp sweetener
salt and freshly ground black pepper
1tsp smoked paprika

4 bacon medallions (all fat removed)
4 x 40g of low fat cheddar cheese
4 x 60g wholemeal rolls
1tbsp fat free fromage frais

Steps

In a pan mix passata, Worcestershire sauce, balsamic vinegar, mustard powder, garlic, smoked paprika, sweetener and seasoning. Bring to the boil and leave to simmer for around 10 minutes on a low heat. Leave to reduce. Add 2tbsp Worcestershire sauce to the beef mince with salt and pepper and combine.

Spray some low calorie spray in a frying pan and heat. Finely chop the bacon and fry-off with the onions until crispy. Remove from heat and put on a paper towel to cool.

Once cooled mix with the cheese, fat free fromage frais, bacon and onions. Form a spoonful of bacon-cheese mixture into a ball and place in the centre of 4 patties. Fold the mixture around to seal and form your burgers.

Cook on a medium heat in a frying pan or griddle. Grill burgers over medium-high heat, flipping once until cooked (about 4 minutes each side for a medium burger) Place in a bun and top with BBQ sauce.

Notes

This recipe makes 4 delicious, ooz, melt in the middle burgers.

STUFFED BACON & ONION BURGERS

These burgers are really easy to make and guaranteed to be a hit with all the family.

This recipe makes 4 burgers and when served to my guests were described as "INCREDIBLE!".

When you bite into the middle of the burger, the flavour of the delicious gooey filling comes out.

BBQ CHICKEN CASSEROLE

PREP TIME
10 minutes

COOK TIME
3 hours

READY IN
3 hours 10
minutes

SERVINGS
4 servings

CALORIES
346 Kcal serving

SOURCE
Sugar Pink Food

Ingredients

300g potatoes, peeled and chopped into cubes
40g extra light cheddar cheese per person
4 rashers of cooked, smoky bacon, all fat removed

For the sauce:
1tbsp mustard powder
pinch of salt and pepper
low calorie cooking spray
1 red onion, finely chopped
1 red pepper, finely chopped
4 large skinless chicken breasts
1tsp mustard powder
For the potatoes:

5tbsp Worcestershire shire sauce
500g passata
3tbsp balsamic vinegar
2 cloves of garlic, crushed
3tbsp sweetener
salt and pepper
1 red onion, diced

Steps

Mix passata, Worcestershire sauce, balsamic vinegar, mustard powder, garlic, sweetener and seasoning.. Chop a red onion and layer on the bottom of your slow cooker.

Add the chicken and BBQ sauce and leave on high for 3 hours. Alternatively you can cook in the oven on a low heat for 1½ hours.

Pull the meat apart with 2 forks and mix with the excess sauce. When ready to make up the casserole, boil the potatoes in salted water to make the mash. Once cooked through, drain and use a masher to make a smooth mashed potato mix.

Add the mustard powder, onions, peppers, salt and pepper and mix well.

Lightly spray a 9" x 13" casserole dish with low calorie cooking spray, then add the mashed potato to make the base. Spread evenly and press down.

Top with the pulled chicken mix, then 40g extra light cheese per person (I weigh 40g at a time and sprinkle on each quarter of the casserole). Top with chopped cooked bacon and a few chillies.

Place in the oven until the cheese has melted and is bubbling.

Notes
I love anything involving BBQ sauce and cheese, and this is one of my personal favourites!
SUGAR PINK FOOD RECIPES

SLOW COOKER RAMEN NOODLE SOUP

PREP TIME
10 minutes

COOK TIME
3 hours

READY IN
3 hours 10 minutes

SERVINGS
4 servings

CALORIES
177 Kcal serving

SOURCE
Sugar Pink Food

Ingredients

2 skinless chicken breasts
700ml chicken stock (made up from cubes)
2 garlic cloves, finely chopped
4tbsp soy sauce
1tsp Worcestershire shire sauce
½tsp pureed ginger
½tsp Chinese five spice
a pinch of dried chilli flakes
125g dried noodles
a pinch of black pepper
½ tin of sweetcorn
1 soft boiled egg
1 bag stir fry vegetables

Steps

Add everything except the noodles into the slow cooker.

Cover and cook on low for 3 hours.

Remove the chicken and set aside. Add the dried noodles to the slow cooker and put the lid back on for a further 10 minutes.

Slice the chicken breasts into strips and after the 10 minutes add to the ramen.

Stir through the chicken and place in bowls to serve.

Top with a soft boiled egg, sliced in half.

Notes

This is a kind of 'cheats' version where I put it in the slow cooker and leave it alone. I save loads of time by getting a stir fry vegetable mix as it has all the perfect items for Ramen.

CHICKEN FAJITA MIX

PREP TIME
10 minutes

COOK TIME
15 minutes

READY IN
25 minutes

SERVINGS
4 servings

CALORIES
182 Kcal serving

SOURCE
Sugar Pink Food

Ingredients

4 large chicken breasts

1 red pepper, chopped

1 yellow pepper, chopped

1 red onion, dice

1tsp smoked paprika

1tsp cumin

2 fresh red chillies, deseeded and finely chopped

1tsp chilli powder

juice of 1 lime

1 clove garlic, crushed

2tbsp tomato purée

Steps

Heat a frying pan over a medium heat and spray with Frylight.

Fry-off the onions, chillies and pepper.

Chop the chicken into bite sized pieces. Add to the pan and sprinkle over the paprika, cumin, chilli powder, lime juice, garlic. Stir fry for 2 minutes.

Add the tomato purée and continue to stir fry until the chicken is cooked all the way through. Add a little water if needed to create more of a sauce.

Notes

This fajita chicken can be used as the filling of a fajita, or can be eaten cold with lunches. I love to make up a batch and keep it in the fridge.

CAJUN CHICKEN TRAYBAKE

PREP TIME
10 minutes

COOK TIME
30 minutes

READY IN
40 minutes

SERVINGS
4 servings

CALORIES
191 Kcal serving

SOURCE
Sugar Pink Food

Ingredients

4 skinless chicken breasts
6tsp smoked paprika
1tsp salt
2tsp ground black pepper
2tsp ground white pepper
2tsp garlic powder
2tsp onion powder
1tsp dried thyme
1tsp cayenne
2tbsp balsamic vinegar
1 large sweet potato, finely chopped
1 carrot, finely chopped
1 red onion, finely chopped
1 lemon or lime

Steps

Preheat the oven to 180°C.

Chop the chicken breasts into bite sized chunks.

Mix together the paprika, black pepper, white pepper, garlic powder, onion powder, thyme, cayenne, balsamic vinegar and the juice of half the lemon.

Pour half of this mixture over the chicken chunks.

Lay out the chopped and prepared vegetables on a baking tray.

Cover with the other half of the Cajun seasoning, and top with the chicken.

Bake in the oven for 25-30 minutes, or until the chicken is cooked through.

Notes

I love weeknight recipes that allow me to chuck everything all in at once, and put it in the slow cooker or oven. This dish only really requires some basic chopping with some seasoning, and a baking tray!

CAJUN CHICKEN TRAYBAKE

I know how hard it can be to get the energy together to cook when you have been at work all day.

That's why I always try and focus on making things as simple and as easy as possible for myself.

I love weeknight recipes that allow me to chuck everything all in at once, and put it in the slow cooker or oven.

This dish only really requires some basic chopping with some seasoning, and a baking tray!

PORK MEATBALLS IN GRAVY

PREP TIME
10 minutes

COOK TIME
40 minutes

READY IN
50 minutes

SERVINGS
4 servings

CALORIES
390 Kcal serving

SOURCE
Sugar Pink Food

Ingredients

For the gravy:
1 large red onion sliced
2 cloves of garlic, crushed
700ml beef stock, can be made up from cubes
1tbsp of balsamic vinegar
1tbsp Worcestershire sauce
1 level tbsp of tomato purée
low calorie cooking spray
salt and black pepper
1tbsp fat free fromage frais
½tsp Italian dried herbs
For the meatballs:
400g 5% fat pork mince
salt and pepper
1tsp smoked paprika
1tsp garlic powder
For the meal:
1 red pepper, finely diced
1 yellow pepper, finely diced
1 onion, finely diced
pasta to serve

Steps

Spray a saucepan with low calorie cooking spray. Add the onions and the garlic, and fry-off for 3-4 minutes over a medium heat, stirring constantly. If anything starts to stick, use some of the stock to loosen it up from the bottom of the pan.

Add the herbs, stock, balsamic vinegar, Worcestershire sauce, tomato purée, low calorie cooking spray, salt and black pepper. Reduce the heat to low, cover and leave to simmer for 30 minutes. Meanwhile, prepare the meatballs. In a bowl, add the pork mince, pinch of salt and pepper, smoked paprika and garlic powder. Mix well. Grab about 1tbsp of pork mixture, then roll into a ball using your hands. Repeat until all the pork mixture has been used.

When the gravy is about 10 minutes from ready, heat a frying pan. Fry-off the peppers and onion. Once cooked, set aside.

Reduce the heat and then add the meatballs to the frying pan. Cook for about 3 minutes on each side. When the gravy is fully cooked, remove and blitz in a blender until completely smooth. Pour the gravy over the meatballs, then add the peppers and onion. Mix well and then stir through the fat free fromage frais before serving. Serve with pasta and a salad.

Notes

Classic home-made comfort food! These meatballs come in a delicious gravy, which is perfect for pasta.

SUGAR PINK FOOD RECIPES

JAMAICAN CHICKEN STEW

PREP TIME
10 minutes

COOK TIME
3 hours

READY IN
3 hours 10
minutes

SERVINGS
4 servings

CALORIES
355 Kcal serving

SOURCE
Sugar Pink Food

Ingredients

large skinless chicken breasts
4 garlic cloves minced
1tbsp Jerk seasoning (try and use a
sugar free one)
a pinch of black pepper
½tsp minced ginger
a handful of fresh thyme
4tbsp Worcestershire shire sauce
2 large onions finely diced
a handful of baby corn, sliced
3 large carrots sliced
1 tin chopped tomatoes
1tbsp allspice
½tsp chilli powder
400ml beef stock made with 2 cubes
and 400ml boiling water
juice of 1 lime

Steps

For best results, sprinkle the chicken
with jerk seasoning the night before
cooking.

Add all the ingredients for the stew into
the slow cooker dish.

Mix well and cook on low for 6 hours,
or high for 3 hours.

If you would rather cook it in the oven,
add all the ingredients to a large
casserole dish and cook on a low heat
for 2 hours.

Make sure you check the chicken is
cooked through.

Notes

Jerk is a style of cooking native to Jamaica in which meat is dry-rubbed or wet
marinated with a hot spice mixture called Jamaican jerk spice.

EASY CHICKEN BAKE

PREP TIME
10 minutes

COOK TIME
1 hour

READY IN
1 hour 10
minutes

SERVINGS
4 servings

CALORIES
390 Kcal serving

SOURCE
Sugar Pink Food

Ingredients

6 skinless, boneless free-range
chicken breasts

2 red onions, sliced

1 red pepper, sliced

1 yellow pepper, sliced

4 large tomatoes, sliced

4 cloves of garlic, finely chopped

1tsp smoked paprika

low calorie cooking spray

2tbsp balsamic vinegar

1tsp cayenne pepper

a large handful of new potatoes,
quartered

salt and pepper

Steps

Preheat the oven to 180ºC.

Put everything, apart from the low
calorie cooking spray, in a large baking
tray.

Mix all the ingredients together and
coat in the vinegar and seasonings.

Spray with Frylight and bake in the
oven for 1 hour, or until the chicken
and vegetables are cooked through.

Serve with a crisp fresh salad.

Notes

This is, as the title suggests, a very easy recipe. With minimal effort, maximum
flavour and very little washing up, it is the perfect weeknight meal. It is packed
with vegetables and goes perfectly with a fresh salad.

EASY CHICKEN BAKE

This is, as the title suggests, a very easy recipe. With minimal effort, maximum flavour and very little washing up, it is the perfect weeknight meal.

It is packed with vegetables and goes perfectly with a fresh salad.

Throw as many vegetables as you possibly can into this dish!

GARLIC CHICKEN BREAST

PREP TIME
10 minutes

COOK TIME
25 minutes

READY IN
35 minutes

SERVINGS
4 servings

CALORIES
462 Kcal serving

SOURCE
Sugar Pink Food

Ingredients

2 large chicken breasts

150g mushrooms, sliced

2 garlic cloves puréed or finely diced

2tbsp extra light spread

salt and pepper

smoked paprika

4 large sweet potatoes, peeled and cut into wedges

salad to serve

1tsp Italian herbs

Steps

Preheat the oven to 200ºC/400ºF/gas 6.

In a large bowl combine sweet potatoes, smoked paprika, salt and pepper. Spray with low calorie cooking spray.

Place each chicken breast on a large square of tin foil. Combine the spread with the garlic, herbs, salt and pepper.

Top each chicken breast with mushrooms. Add 1tbs of the garlic butter to each chicken breast and then fold the tin foil to make a parcel around each breast. Place on a baking tray.

Spread the wedges out on a large baking tray. Cook both the chicken breasts for 35 minutes. Make sure you check that the chicken breasts are cooked all the way through before serving. Serve with a large side salad.

Notes

This is a proper weeknight meal, simple and quick to make. It goes perfectly with sweet potato chips or my garlic bread flavour chips!

MEXICAN TURKEY STEAKS

PREP TIME
10 minutes

COOK TIME
35 minutes

READY IN
45 minutes

SERVINGS
2 steaks

CALORIES
290 Kcal serving

SOURCE
Sugar Pink Food

Ingredients

1tsp chili powder (add more if you like)
1tsp garlic powder
1tsp onion powder (or 2tsp crushed dried fried onions)
½tsp crushed red pepper flakes
½tsp dried oregano
2tsp smoked paprika
1½tsp ground cumin
½tsp sea salt
½tsp black pepper
a pinch of ground cinnamon
1 chicken stock cube, crushed
1 turkey steak per person serving
1 tin of Tesco taco mixed beans, canned

Steps

Mix together the chilli powder, garlic powder, onion powder, red flakes, oregano, smoked paprika, cumin, salt and pepper together. Add the juice of half the lemon to create a paste.

Spray the turkey steaks with low calorie cooking spray and coat in the spice paste, leave to marinate in the fridge for at least 30 minutes.

Heat a griddle or frying pan over a medium heat, fry-off the turkey steaks, ensuring that they are cooked all the way through, turning regularly.

Heat the tin of taco beans, and serve over a salad with a lime to squeeze over the turkey steaks.

Notes

Turkey is really lean, so it is a great free meat and nice to have something other than chicken. This dish has a spicy kick, so make sure you taste the spice mix before cooking with it!

CREAMY CHICKEN PIE

PREP TIME
10 minutes

COOK TIME
25 minutes

READY IN
35 minutes

SERVINGS
4 servings

CALORIES
345 Kcal serving

SOURCE
Sugar Pink Food

Ingredients

100ml chicken stock

2 skinless chicken breasts, chopped

2 onions, chopped

1 garlic clove, finely chopped

200g chopped mushrooms

1tbsp smoked paprika

1 level tsp chicken gravy granules

2tbsp fat free fromage frais

2tbsp Quark

4 medallions of smoked bacon

Salt and freshly ground black pepper

1 egg, lightly beaten

112g ready-to-roll light puff pastry

Steps

Preheat the oven to 180°C.

Place the stock, bacon, chicken, onions, garlic, paprika and mushrooms in a pan. Cook over a medium heat for 10 minutes or until the onions have softened, and the chicken and bacon have cooked through.

Add the gravy granules and stir well. Remove from the heat and add seasoning, Quark and fromage frais. Allow to cool.

Place the pie dish top down on the pastry and cut around to make the top.

Brush the lips of the dishes with some of the beaten egg and fill the dish with the chicken filling. Top with the pastry and brush with the rest of the beaten egg over the pastry.

Cook for 18-20 minutes or until the pastry is cooked and golden.

Notes

If there's one thing I love, it's a good old pie! I have now discovered lower calorie pastry. This means that lower calorie pies are possible!

SUGAR PINK FOOD RECIPES

CREAMY CHICKEN PIE

If there's one thing I love, it's a good old pie! I have now discovered lower calorie pastry. This means that pies are possible when trying to eat healthy or lose weight!

This pie even has a delicious, creamy filling that you wouldn't even realise is healthier!

BEEF & MAPLE MEATBALLS

PREP TIME
10 minutes

COOK TIME
3 hours

READY IN
3 hours 10
minutes

SERVINGS
4 servings

CALORIES
365 Kcal serving

SOURCE
Sugar Pink Food

Ingredients

500g lean beef mince
1 red pepper, finely chopped
1tsp Italian herbs
1 red onion, finely chopped
2 cloves of garlic, crushed
a pinch of salt and black pepper
1 carrot, peeled and grated
½ a fresh or dried red chilli
1 sweet potato, peeled, cut into small
chunks
500g of passata
½ litre beef stock
2tbsp balsamic vinegar
3tbsp low sugar Maple flavour syrup
low calorie cooking spray

Steps

In a large bowl mix the mince, half the minced garlic, salt and pepper. Using your hands, mix all the ingredients together well. Roll into 12 even meatballs.

Spray a frying pan with low calorie cooking spray and fry-off the meatballs until they are browned on the outside and sealed.

Add the meatballs with the rest of the ingredients to the slow cooker and leave for 3 hours on high or 6 hours on low.

Notes

I love trying out new flavours and getting inspiration from things I see on TV. I heard about a tomato and maple sauce with meatballs, and had to try one out for myself.

SUGAR PINK FOOD RECIPES

CHILLI & MANGO CHICKEN BREAST

PREP TIME
10 minutes

COOK TIME
35 minutes

READY IN
45 minutes

SERVINGS
4 servings

CALORIES
290 Kcal serving

SOURCE
Sugar Pink Food

Ingredients

100ml Rubicon mango juice

4tbsp sweet chilli sauce

2tbsp soy sauce

2tsp minced ginger

1tsp minced garlic

1 red chilli, thinly sliced, optional

4 skinless, boneless chicken breasts
mini fillets

salt and pepper

1tsp smoked paprika

Steps

In a large bowl mix together all the ingredients for the chicken.

Cover and leave to marinate overnight or for at least 30 minutes.

Preheat a grill to high heat. Arrange the breasts on a foil lined tray.

Baste with any left over marinade and cook for 8-10 minutes on either side.

Notes

This fragrant chicken dish is perfect for summer BBQs (and even indoor grills when the great British weather lets us down!). It pairs perfectly with a salad and spicy rice.

SIZZLING BEEF FAJITA

PREP TIME
10 minutes

COOK TIME
10 minutes

READY IN
20 minutes

SERVINGS
4 servings

CALORIES
340 Kcal serving

SOURCE
Sugar Pink Food

Ingredients

4 lean "sizzle steaks" (thin) sliced into strips
1tbsp Worcestershire sauce
Frylight
1 red pepper, seeds removed, cut into strips
1 yellow pepper, seeds removed, cut into strips
1 red onion, finely sliced
1tsp smoked paprika
1tsp cumin
2 fresh red chillies, de-seeded and finely chopped
1tsp chilli powder
Juice of 1 lime
1 clove garlic, crushed
2tbsp tomato purée

Steps

Add the peppers, onion, garlic and chillies to a frying pan and cook over a medium heat.

Turn the heat down and add the rest of the ingredients, including the beef.

Stir in the pan and cook for 1-2 minutes for rare steak, or 3-4 minutes to cook it through. Stir to ensure an even coating of herbs and spices across all meat and vegetables.

Serve with your choice of egg wrap, rice or salad.

Notes
If you like fajitas mix then you'll love this sizzling beef recipe! Easy to whip up in a frying pan or skillet and can be served in egg wraps, with salad or simply with rice.

CHICKEN PARMIGIANA CASSEROLE

PREP TIME
10 minutes

COOK TIME
30 minutes

READY IN
40 minutes

SERVINGS
4 servings

CALORIES
325 Kcal serving

SOURCE
Sugar Pink Food

Ingredients

1 bag frozen pre-cooked chicken pieces or 1 pack skinless diced chicken breast
240g wholemeal bread, made into breadcrumbs
2tbsp grated parmesan
2tsp minced garlic
1 carton passata
1tsp sweetener sugar
2tsp mixed herbs
180g ball of mozzarella
low calorie cooking spray
1 beef tomato, sliced

Steps

Preheat the oven to 180°C.

Using a casserole dish, layer with the chicken and pour over the passata. Add the sweetener, garlic and 1tsp of the herbs and mix.

Mix the parmesan, breadcrumbs and the rest of the herbs.

Top the chicken mix with breadcrumbs and layer slices of the beef tomato and mozzarella, careful to give 45g per person if using a healthy extra.

Cook for 20 minutes or until the breadcrumbs have browned and cheese has melted.

Notes

This is a twist on the Chicken Parmigiana, making it in a casserole dish with the breadcrumbs on top.

MINTED LAMB BURGERS

PREP TIME
15 minutes

COOK TIME
20 minutes

READY IN
35 minutes

SERVINGS
4 burgers

CALORIES
212Kcal

SOURCE
Sugar Pink Food

Ingredients

lamb mince 10% fat

1tsp garlic granules

1tsp dried mint

1tsp fresh coriander chopped finely

1tsp granulated sweetener

a pinch of salt and pepper

1tbsp fat free yogurt

Steps

Put the lamb mince in a large bowl.

Add the burger ingredients and mix well with your hands.

Use your hands to form 4 even burger patties. Cover and then play in the fridge for at least 15 minutes.

Heat a frying pan over a medium heat, then add the patties. Cook for around 6 minutes on each side.

Serve in your choice of bun with salad.

Notes

These lamb burgers are succulent, tasty, and full of flavour. Lamb is traditionally quite fatty, so make sure you get reduced fat mince.

INDIAN BUTTER CHICKEN

PREP TIME
10 minutes

COOK TIME
25 minutes

READY IN
35 minutes

SERVINGS
4 servings

CALORIES
524 Kcal serving

SOURCE
Sugar Pink Food

Ingredients

2 cloves of garlic, crushed
2 large onion, finely diced
2tsp of fresh grated ginger
1 carton of passata
200ml of water
2tsp of chilli powder
1tsp of paprika
1tsp of garam masala
¼tsp cayenne pepper
1tbsp of butter
cooking oil spray
4 boneless chicken breast, diced
120ml of fat free plain yogurt
2 cloves of garlic, crushed
2tsp grated fresh ginger
2tsp chilli powder
1tsp paprika
1tsp garam masala
pinch of salt
1tbsp of fat free fromage frais
juice from ½ a lime

Steps

Mix together the yogurt, garlic, ginger, chilli powder, paprika, lime juice, garam masala and a pinch of salt. Add to the chicken and mix to coat.

Marinate overnight in the fridge.

Spray a large pan with low calorie cooking spray.

Add the marinated chicken and cook-off over a medium heat.

Once cooked, remove the chicken and set aside.

Fry-off the onion for a few minutes in the pan. Once they have softened, add garlic, ginger and the spices. Add some water to stop it from drying up.

Add the passata then cook for another 5 minutes.

You can either leave the sauce chunky, or blitz in a blender until smooth.

Add the chicken back to the sauce once blitzed. Stir through the butter and fat free fromage frais before serving..

Notes
Indian is one of the most popular takeaways, and this is my take on a Butter Chicken curry.

MAC & CHILLI CHEESE CON CARNE

PREP TIME
15 minutes

COOK TIME
35 minutes

READY IN
50 minutes

SERVINGS
4 servings

CALORIES
498 Kcal serving

SOURCE
Sugar Pink Food

Ingredients

Low calorie cooking spray
1 large red onion, finely chopped
2 garlic cloves, crushe
1tsp smoked paprika
2 fresh chillies, deseeded and chopped
(adjust to how spicy you want it!)
500g lean beef mince (5% fat or less)
2tsp ground cumin
1tsp ground coriander
300ml beef stock, made up from a stock cube
a pinch of cayenne pepper
1 green pepper and 1 yellow pepper chopped
1 tin chopped tomatoes
salt and freshly ground black pepper
400g tin of red kidney beans
150g dried macaroni pasta
160g of extra light cheese, split into 2 80g piles

Steps

Preheat the oven to 180°C.

Spray a large saucepan with the cooking spray, then add the onion and garlic. Cook until they are softened. Add the beef mince and cook until browned. Add the chillies and spices and stir for a few minutes while cooking.

Add the peppers, tomatoes and stock. Stir, bring to the boil and then reduce to a simmer.

Simmer until the liquid has been reduced.

Add the kidney beans and a pinch of salt and pepper. Leave on a low heat while you cook the pasta.

Parboil the pasta in salted water. Once cooked, drain and then add to the chilli mix.

Add 1 of the 80g piles of cheese to the pasta and chilli mix, and stir through.

Add to an oven proof dish and sprinkle the rest of the cheese on top.

Bake in the oven for 10 minutes or until the cheese on top is bubbling.

Notes

This is a delicious twist on mac & cheese, by adding in a delicious chilli con carne!

DOUBLE CHICKEN BUN BURGER

PREP TIME
10 minutes

COOK TIME
25 minutes

READY IN
35 minutes

SERVINGS
1 burger

CALORIES
479 Kcal burger

SOURCE
Sugar Pink Food

Ingredients

For the chicken:
2 small chicken fillets
2 slices of 400g wholemeal bread
1tsp oregano
1tsp chilli powder
1tsp ground sage
1tsp basil
1tsp pepper
2tsp salt
2tsp paprika
1tsp garlic powder
1tsp garlic salt
1 egg

Cheese slices and cooked bacon
medallions.

Steps

Blitz the bread in a food processor until it is fine breadcrumbs. Put into a bowl and add all of the seasonings. Mix until everything is blended together to create your coating.

Crack the egg into a dish and whisk. The chicken needs to be dipped in the egg and then to the breadcrumb mixture, and repeat to get an even coating.

Tip: Only use one hand for touching the egg and the other hand for touching the breadcrumbs. This stops a sticky mixture on your fingers!

Bake the chicken in the oven for 20-25 minutes on a medium heat. Always check the chicken is cooked all the way through before serving.

Notes
Instead of your usual burger, the bread bun is replaced with 2 bits of chicken, so you have bacon BBQ sauce and cheese sandwiched between the chicken, heaven.

BBQ BACON PASTA

PREP TIME
10 minutes

COOK TIME
20 minutes

READY IN
35 minutes

SERVINGS
4 servings

CALORIES
437 Kcal serving

SOURCE
Sugar Pink Food

Ingredients

5tbsp Worcestershire sauce
6 bacon medallions, all fat removed
1 onion, diced
1 red pepper, finely sliced
½small tin sweetcorn
1tsp mustard powder
500g carton of passata
3tbsp balsamic vinegar
2 cloves of garlic, crushed
3tbsp sweetener
salt and freshly ground black pepper
1tsp smoked paprika
¼pint coke zero
250g dried pasta of your choice
120g light cheese
low-calorie cooking spray

Steps

In a saucepan mix the balsamic vinegar, coke zero and Worcestershire sauce. Bring to the boil and then leave to reduce.

Mix in passata, mustard powder, garlic, smoked paprika, sweetener, and seasoning. Bring to the boil and then allow to simmer for 10-15 minutes until it has thickened and reduced.

Spray a pan with low-calorie cooking spray, and fry-off the bacon, onions and pepper. Parboil the dried pasta for 5 minutes.

Mix the bacon and vegetables with the BBQ sauce and pasta. Add to a shallow pasta bake tray, and mix well. Top with the cheese. Bake for 10-15 minutes, or until the pasta is cooked through and the cheese is bubbling.

Notes
This is a super easy 'throw it all together' meal!

EASY PAELLA

PREP TIME
10 minutes

COOK TIME
25 minutes

READY IN
35 minutes

SERVINGS
4 servings

CALORIES
535 Kcal serving

SOURCE
Sugar Pink Food

Ingredients

1 red pepper, sliced

1 yellow pepper, sliced

1 bunch flat leaf parsley

1 garlic clove

a handful of cherry tomatoes

250g chicken thighs

4 sprigs rosemary

1 chicken stock pot

4 slices chorizo

350g basmati rice

1 lemon

600ml boiling water

Steps

Chop the chicken thighs into bite-sized chunks. Pour the boiling water (amount as stated in the ingredient list) into a jug with chicken stock pot and stir to dissolve. Pull the rosemary leaves from their sprigs. Spray a frying pan with low calorie cooking spray, then turn to a high heat. Season your chicken well with salt and pepper.

Add your chicken to the pan and fry for a few minutes. Once browned on all sides, remove and keep to the side. Add another spray of low calorie cooking spray to the frying pan. Add peppers, tomato, garlic, rosemary and chorizo. After 3 minutes, add the rice and half of your parsley. Cook for a few minutes until your rice absorbs the oil. Add the stock.

Reduce the heat to medium-low and cook for 15-20 minutes. Once the liquid has been soaked up, take your paella off the heat. Cover with a clean tea towel and leave for 5 minutes. Serve with your remaining parsley and big wedges of lemon,

Notes
An extra simple paella recipe that the whole family will love!

EASY PAELLA

Simple rice dishes are proper comfort food to me, and the taste of Paella always reminds me of sunshine and summer.

I love the combination of flavours and colours that come in this dish.

Paella is one of my favourite comfort foods.

CHILLI CON CARNE

PREP TIME
10 minutes

COOK TIME
25 minutes

READY IN
35 minutes

SERVINGS
4 servings

CALORIES
357 Kcal serving

SOURCE
Sugar Pink Food

Ingredients

low calorie cooking spray
1 large red onion, finely chopped
2 garlic cloves, crushed
2 fresh chillies, deseeded and chopped
500g lean beef mince (5% fat or less)
2tsp ground cumin
1tsp ground coriander
1tsp paprika
a pinch of cayenne pepper
1 green pepper and 1 yellow pepper, chopped
4 ripe plum tomatoes, chopped
300ml beef stock
salt and freshly ground black pepper
400g tin of red kidney beans

Steps

Spray a large saucepan with low calorie cooking spray. Fry the onion and garlic gently over a low heat for 5 minutes, until softened and golden. Add the minced beef and cook until browned. Add the chillies and spices and fry for a few minutes.

Add the peppers, tomatoes and stock. Stir well and bring to the boil. Reduce the heat and simmer gently for 15 minutes until the liquid is reduced. Season to taste and add the kidney beans. Cook for a further 5 minutes.

Serve topped with a swirl of fromage frais and sprinkle with chopped herbs and paprika on top of a jacket potato or with lots of rice.

Notes

This classic chilli con carne is a quick and easy recipe that's bursting with fiery flavour.

CHINESE CHICKEN CURRY

PREP TIME
10 minutes

COOK TIME
25 minutes

READY IN
35 minutes

SERVINGS
4 servings

CALORIES
437Kcal

SOURCE
Sugar Pink Food

Ingredients

2 large skinless chicken breasts,
diced
low calorie cooking spray
1 onion, peeled and finely chopped
2 garlic cloves, peeled and crushed
½tsp pureed ginger
½ carton passata
1tsp Chinese five spice
2tbsp sweetener
100g frozen mixed veg
500ml boiling chicken stock
1 level tsp cornflour, mixed with
2tsp cold water
½tsp turmeric
2 star anise
2tsp mild curry powder

Steps

Spray a saucepan with low calorie cooking spray and place over a medium heat. Add the onion and garlic and cook until soft. Add the ginger and cook for 1-2 minutes, then add the curry powder and rest of the spices. Cook for a further 1-2 minutes.

Add the stock and sweetener and passata and bring to the boil. Transfer the sauce to a food processor and blend until smooth. Return to the pan, add vegetables and diced chicken breasts.

Simmer on low for 15 minutes, stirring occasionally. After 15 minutes, remove a piece of chicken and check to make sure it is cooked all the way through before serving. Add cornflour mixed with water to thicken.

Notes

I love a Chinese curry, and this one certainly doesn't disappoint! Works with any meat.

CHINESE CHICKEN CURRY

I love a good Chinese Chicken Curry, and often make mine from scratch. Sometimes it is much easier to throw all the ingredients together without having to really think much about cooking!

PHILLY CHEESESTEAK FRIES

PREP TIME
10 minutes

COOK TIME
25 minutes

READY IN
35 minutes

SERVINGS
4 servings

CALORIES
365 Kcal serving

SOURCE
Sugar Pink Food

Ingredients

2-4 minute steaks, thinly sliced with all visible fat removed (1 for each person you are cooking for)
low calorie cooking spray
salt and freshly ground black pepper
a large handful of mushrooms
1 green pepper
1 yellow pepper
1 large red onion
1tbsp Balsamic vinegar
1tbsp Worcestershire sauce
500g medium sized Maris Piper potatoes

a pinch of cayenne pepper
1tsp smoked paprika
40g extra light cheddar
40g extra light red Leicester
a few sliced jalapenos to top

Steps

Preheat oven to 220°C. Peel the potatoes. Slice lengthwise into approx 1cm thick rectangular chips.

Bring a large saucepan of salted water to the boil. Add the chips and cook for 4 minutes. Rough chips up by putting back in the sauce pan with the lid on and shaking it.

Spray a metal baking tray with low calorie cooking spray. Transfer the chips to the tray, spray lightly with low calorie cooking spray and bake in the oven for 30 minutes, turning occasionally, until golden brown on all sides. While the chips are in the oven, prepare the philly cheese steak topping. Thinly slice the onions, peppers and mushrooms and fry-off until cooked through. Add the steak, salt and pepper, Worcestershire sauce, balsamic vinegar, pinch of cayenne pepper, and smoked paprika. Fry-off and mix everything together for 1 minute for rare steak or 2 minutes for well done.

Add chips in an oven proof bowl and top with the steak and vegetables, and then the cheese, remembering that you are allowed 40g per person as a healthy extra. Put in the oven for 3-4 minutes until the cheese has melted.

Notes

Thinly-sliced pieces of steak and melted cheese on top of crispy baked fries.

JAMBALAYA

PREP TIME
10 minutes

COOK TIME
3 hours

READY IN
3 hours 10
minutes

SERVINGS
4 servings

CALORIES
537 Kcal serving

SOURCE
Sugar Pink Food

Ingredients

1 red onion, diced
3 garlic cloves, crushed
1 red pepper, 1 green pepper and 1
yellow pepper, chopped into chunks
1 courgette, chopped into chunks
4 skinless chicken breasts, chopped
into chunks
1 x 400g tin chopped tomatoes
2tbsp dried thyme
2tbsp fresh parsley
1tsp smoked paprika
1tsp cayenne pepper
1 bay leaf
350g long grain rice, dried
1l chicken stock
salt and freshly ground black pepper
sliced lemon to serve

Steps

In the slow cooker, mix all the
ingredients together apart from the rice.

Cover and cook for 7-8 hours on low or
for 3-4 hours on high.

Stir in the rice for the last hour of
cooking, keep an eye on it to make sure
it doesn't stick to the bottom, stir
occasionally.

Notes

Jambalaya comes from America's Deep South and combines elements of
Spanish and French cooking, and I believe it is one of the best comfort food
dishes!

BBQ BEAN BAKE

PREP TIME
10 minutes

COOK TIME
25 minutes

READY IN
35 minutes

SERVINGS
4 servings

CALORIES
170 Kcal serving

SOURCE
Sugar Pink Food

Ingredients

1 red onion, diced
2 garlic cloves, chopped
1tbsp white wine vinegar
1 tin pinto beans, drained and rinsed
1 tin kidney beans, drained and rinsed
400ml tub passata
1tsp Worcestershire sauce
3tbsp balsamic vinegar
3tbsp sweetener
Salt and pepper
1tsp smoked paprika
40g extra light cheese/35g smoked cheddar per portion

Steps

Fry-off the onion and garlic until softened. Add all the rest of the bean ingredients, and mix well.

Transfer into an ovenproof dish and bake for 35 minutes, or until everything has softened.

Top with the cheese, then put back in the oven until melted.

Notes

I love anything BBQ flavour, and this is so tasty that you won't even know that it is relatively healthy

BBQ BEAN BAKE

You can kind of throw in the ingredients, and this recipe would also come out great in a slow cooker.

I love anything BBQ flavour, and this is so tasty that you won't even know that it is relatively healthy!

PERI PERI CHICKEN KEBAB

PREP TIME
10 minutes

COOK TIME
4 hours

READY IN
4 hours 10
minutes

SERVINGS
4 servings

CALORIES
203 Kcal serving

SOURCE
Sugar Pink Food

Ingredients

9 boneless, skinless chicken thighs
2 birds-eye red chillies (adjust according
to personal taste, the more chillies the
hotter it is!)
1 red pepper
1 red onion
juice of 1 lemon
juice of ½ a lime
1tbsp smoked paprika
2tsp salt
1tsp black pepper
1tbsp oregano
½tsp red chilli powder
5 cloves of garlic
4tbsp malt vinegar
4 cherry tomatoes
50ml water
To serve: wholemeal pitta bread

Steps

Blitz all the peri peri sauce ingredients together in a food processor until it becomes a smooth paste. Use this to marinate the chicken and to cook it in. Pour the marinade over the chicken and leave to marinate overnight for best flavour, or at least a few hours.

Use a potato and cut the side of one of the long edges off, so it sits flat. Stick in 3 kebab sticks, in a triangle shape.

I cooked mine in the slow cooker, so trimmed the sticks down to make sure they weren't higher than the lid. You could also cook this in the oven (see notes). I made one of the sticks a little longer, so I could lean it against the top of the slow cooker, so it slanted to the side. I moved halfway through cooking.

Use the 3 kebab sticks to build up the kebab. Thread each marinated chicken mini fillet onto the skewers. Press down firmly to get the kebab shape. Cook in the slow cooker for 4 hours on low.

Remove from the slow cooker, and then slice down the side of the kebab to get your meat chunks.

Serve with wholemeal pittas and salad.

Notes
I really enjoy the deliciousness and ease of making a chicken kebab in the slow cooker. Or just cook in the oven for 45 minutes instead.

SUGAR PINK FOOD RECIPES

SIMPLE MUSHROOM RISOTTO

PREP TIME
10 minutes

COOK TIME
25 minutes

READY IN
35 minutes

SERVINGS
4 servings

CALORIES
155 Kcal serving

SOURCE
Sugar Pink Food

Ingredients

1 onion finely chopped

½ litre of hot chicken stock (can be made up from a cube)

135g of Arborio rice

100g of mushrooms (I used baby mushrooms)

1 clove of garlic (crushed)

pinch dried thyme

salt and black pepper

Optional: 1tbsp fat-free fromage frais

Optional: crispy bacon to serve

Steps

Place the stock in a small saucepan with the thyme. Add to a low heat.

Spray a frying pan with low-calorie cooking spray. Add the onion, garlic and mushrooms and cook until softened and golden.

Add a little of the stock if needed to prevent it from sticking.

Season with a pinch of black pepper.

Add the Arborio rice and mix thoroughly with the onion, garlic and mushrooms.

Add 1 ladle of stock and stir. Stir it often, but feel free to give your arms (and the rice) a break if you need to.

As the stock reduces, add another ladle of stock, and repeat the process until all of the stock has been used and the rice is cooked through.

Stir through the fat-free fromage frais to add extra creaminess.

Notes

Is there anything better than an easy mushroom risotto? Perfect as a starter or main, the luxurious and creamy dish is a winner.

SUGAR PINK FOOD RECIPES

CHICKEN TIKKA STIR FRY RICE

PREP TIME
10 minutes

COOK TIME
25 minutes

READY IN
35 minutes

SERVINGS
4 servings

CALORIES
347 Kcal serving

SOURCE
Sugar Pink Food

Ingredients

6tbsp Tikka curry powder
juice of 1 lime
500g diced skinless chicken breast
2tbsp fat free natural yogurt
200g long grain rice, cooked and cooled
1 red pepper sliced
1 yellow pepper, sliced
1 red onion diced
2tsp smoked paprika
1tsp minced garlic
1 chicken stock cube, dissolved in 125 ml water
3tbsp tomato puree
low calorie cooking spray

Steps

Mix 3 tablespoons of tikka curry powder with the natural yogurt. Add in the diced chicken and mix until coated. Leave in the fridge for at least 20 minutes, or overnight if you can.

Spray a large frying pan with low calorie cooking spray, then fry the onion and pepper until softened. Add in the garlic, and the other 3 tablespoons of tikka curry powder and smoked paprika.

Add in the marinated chicken, and cook through.

Add in the stock, rice and tomato puree. Mix well and allow to simmer until the stock has soaked into the rice.

Notes

Sometimes, the most delicious meals come about from throwing together what you have in the cupboard. That is very much how this dish was created.

CRISPY CHILLI BEEF

PREP TIME
20 minutes

COOK TIME
30 minutes

READY IN
50 minutes

SERVINGS
4 servings

CALORIES
302 Kcal serving

SOURCE
Sugar Pink Food

Ingredients

500g lean rump steak, cut into strips
200ml beef stock (can be made up
from a cube)
2tbsp sweet chilli sauce
2tbsp tomato puree
2tbsp Worcestershire sauce
1tbsp clear honey
1tbsp lemon juice
½tsp ginger paste
2tbsp cornflour
1 red pepper deseeded and sliced
½onion sliced
5 spring onions chopped
1tsp chilli flakes
sea salt and freshly ground black
pepper

Steps

Switch your oven on to 180 degrees.

Flatten out your rump steak, and cut into thin strips. Coat each strip in cornflour, and then lay them out on the Zanussi AirFry tray. Cook in the oven for 10 minutes. Thanks to the Zanussi tray, there's no need to turn the strips halfway through.

Slice up the carrot, onion, garlic, pepper and add to a frying pan. Add the ginger and fry on a low temperature for approximately 5 minutes.

Make the sauce coating by mixing the sweet chilli sauce, tomato puree, chilli flakes, Worcestershire sauce, clear honey, lemon juice and a little of the stock until it creates a glaze.

When the strips have been in for 10 minutes, remove them from the oven. Drop them into the bowl with the sauce and mix around. Place the strips back on the tray and cook for another 5 minutes. Add the rest of the sauce to the pan with the carrots and peppers and cook for the 5 minutes the strips are in the oven.

Remove the strips and add them to the pan with the peppers, onions and carrots. Mix well.

Sprinkle on the spring onions to serve.

Notes

Crispy Chilli Beef is a classic Chinese takeaway dish that I absolutely love. This can also be easily created at home with very little effort.

SPICY VODKA PASTA

PREP TIME
5 minutes

COOK TIME
25 minutes

READY IN
30 minutes

SERVINGS
4 servings

CALORIES
266 Kcal serving

SOURCE
Sugar Pink Food

Ingredients

1 clove of garlic, diced

1 red onion, finely diced

2tbsp tomato puree

100g low fat cream cheese (can be swapped for quark to remove even more fat, and remove 8 syns)

1tbsp vodka

¼ of a red chilli, finely diced

200g grams of dried penne pasta

60g parmesan cheese

salt and pepper to taste

low calorie cooking spray

Steps

Cook the pasta as per the pack instructions, in a pan of boiling water.

Spray a large saucepan with low calorie cooking spray.

Add the onion and garlic to the large saucepan and cook until softened, over a medium heat.

Add the tomato paste and stir.

Add in the cream cheese, and stir until it has all melted. Add the vodka, stir and keep cooking. Add in the chilli.

Keep stirring until combined. Season with salt and pepper. Remove sauce from the heat.

Cook the pasta separately.

When the pasta is cooked, save 1/4 of the pasta water before draining. Add the pasta and the pasta water to the sauce. Stir well until it is all combined.

Add some more salt and pepper, and serve with the rest of the parmesan on top.

Notes

I absolutely love pasta dishes, especially finding new ones. This one has a really unique flavour, which is delicious!

SUGAR PINK FOOD RECIPES

HUNTERS CHICKEN PASTA

PREP TIME
10 minutes

COOK TIME
40 minutes

READY IN
50 minutes

SERVINGS
4 servings

CALORIES
588 Kcal serving

SOURCE
Sugar Pink Food

Ingredients

2 large skinless chicken breasts,
diced into small chunks
5tbsp Worcestershire sauce
6 bacon medallions, all fat removed
1 onion, diced
1 red pepper, finely sliced
½ small tin sweetcorn
1tsp mustard powder
500g carton of tomato passata
3tbsp balsamic vinegar
2 cloves of garlic, crushed
3tbsp sweetener
salt and ground black pepper
1tsp smoked paprika
¼ pint coke zero
250g dried pasta of your choice
120g light cheese
low calorie cooking spray

Steps

Preheat the oven to 180°C. In a saucepan add the balsamic vinegar, coke zero and Worcestershire sauce. Bring to the boil and then leave to reduce.

Mix in passata, mustard powder, garlic, smoked paprika, sweetener, and seasoning. Bring to the boil and then allow to simmer for 10-15 mins until it has thickened and reduced.

Spray a frying pan with low-calorie cooking spray, and fry off the bacon, onions, and pepper.

Add the diced chicken breast to the pan. I like to add an extra pinch of smoked paprika at this stage to give the chicken an extra kick. Par-boil the dried pasta for 5 minutes.

Mix the cooked chicken, bacon and vegetables, mix with the BBQ sauce and pasta, but set some BBQ sauce aside to go on top of the cheese.

Add to a shallow pasta bake tray, and mix well. Top with the cheese. Bake for 10 to 15 minutes, or until the pasta is cooked through and the cheese is bubbling.

Notes

BBQ sauce, cheese and pasta are an amazing combination! Proper comfort food vibes, and this dish is just perfect!

CREAMY SPINACH & PARMESAN CHICKEN

PREP TIME
10 minutes

COOK TIME
20 minutes

READY IN
30 minutes

SERVINGS
4 servings

CALORIES
327 Kcal serving

SOURCE
Sugar Pink Food

Ingredients

4 chicken breasts
a pinch salt and pepper
1tsp oregano
1 onion, finely diced
4 cloves garlic, finely diced
1 small jar sun-dried tomatoes, drained from oil, rinsed and chopped
120ml chicken stock (can be made up from a cube)
120ml low-fat double cream
60g grated parmesan cheese
½ large bag of spinach
large handful of mushrooms, finely sliced

Steps

Season each chicken breast with salt, pepper and oregano.

Spray a large pan with low-calorie cooking spray. Add the chicken breasts and cook for about 4 minutes on each side until browned.

Once cooked through, remove and set aside.

Add some more low-calorie spray to the pan, then add the mushrooms, onion, garlic, and sundried tomatoes.

Slowly add chicken stock, double cream, and parmesan cheese. Mix well to combine until smooth over a low heat.

Add salt and pepper seasoning. Add in the spinach and cook until wilted.

Add the chicken breasts back to the pan and reheat for 2-3 minutes.

I served mine with some brown rice. Serve the creamy chicken with spinach and parmesan sauce immediately, garnished with fresh chopped parsley.

Notes

Chicken with a creamy parmesan sauce, tomatoes and spinach. A real creamy and delicious treat!

CREAMY MUSHROOM PASTA

PREP TIME
10 minutes

COOK TIME
20 minutes

READY IN
30 minutes

SERVINGS
4 servings

CALORIES
258 Kcal serving

SOURCE
Sugar Pink Food

Ingredients

1 onion, finely diced

100ml vegetable stock made up from a cube

1 yellow pepper, finely diced

250g mushrooms, sliced

1 garlic clove, finely grated

1/2 tub extra light cream cheese

300g pasta of your choice

½tsp dried Italian herbs

Salt and pepper

Steps

Spray a frying pan with low calorie cooking spray, and add in the mushrooms, onion and pepper. Cook for approximately 10 minutes over a medium heat.

Add the garlic and cook for 2 minutes.

Add the stock and reduce to a simmer.

Add in the extra light cream cheese (or quark) and keep on the lowest heat while stirring through. Season with salt and black pepper.

Meanwhile, cook the pasta following pack instructions. Reserve 100ml of the pasta water.

Add the cooked pasta in the pan with the creamy sauce, and add a little bit of the reserved water to loosen and create your creamy sauce.

Notes

A simple, easy and vegetarian pasta dish that the whole family will love.

CHICKEN, SWEET POTATO & SPINACH BAKE

PREP TIME
15 minutes

COOK TIME
40 minutes

READY IN
45 minutes

SERVINGS
4 servings

CALORIES
341 Kcal serving

SOURCE
Sugar Pink Food

Ingredients

2 large skinless chicken breasts, diced (or diced chicken)
2 sweet potatoes, peeled and diced
10 mushrooms, sliced
1 red onion, diced
1 chicken oxo cube (separate from the stock)
2 garlic cloves, minced
a large handful baby spinach
100ml chicken stock (can be made up from stock cube)
½ pack low fat cream cheese (or use quark to save calories/syns)
1tbsp garlic powder
1tbsp onion powder
1tbsp smoked paprika
sea salt and freshly ground black pepper

Steps

Preheat the oven to 180°C.

In a bowl, mix the garlic powder, onion powder and paprika, the chicken stock cube, crumbled up, then a large pinch of salt and pepper. Sprinkle this mix over the diced chicken.

Spray a frying pan with low calorie cooking spray, and brown the chicken for 2-3 mins each side. Once done, remove the chicken and add it to your baking dish. Add the sweet potatoes to the pan you used to cook the chicken, and fry for 3 minutes.

Add the onion, mushrooms, and garlic to the sweet potatoes and cook for another 2 to 3 minutes. Turn off the heat, then add the stock and the cream cheese, and mix until the cheese has melted. Add more stock if it looks too thick, or more cream cheese if it looks too thin.

Pour this mix over the chicken, then top with the spinach.

Place in the oven and bake for 18 to 20 minutes.

Notes

A delicious low syn Slimming World friendly chicken bake recipe with chicken, sweet potato and spinach.

SIDE RECIPES

GARLIC BREAD CHIPS

PREP TIME
10 minutes

COOK TIME
30 minutes

READY IN
40 minutes

SERVINGS
4 servings

CALORIES
290 Kcal serving

SOURCE
Sugar Pink Food

Ingredients

1 tsp of garlic granules

a generous pinch of salt and pepper

½ tsp dried parsley

low calorie cooking spray

Steps

Preheat the oven to 220°C.

Peel the potatoes and slice them into chip shapes.

Parboil the chips for 5 minutes in a pan of boiling water. Drain the water and then shake the chips up in the pan to rough them up.

Add the garlic, salt, pepper and parsley to the chips. Spray them all over with low calorie cooking spray, and mix up to cover them in the flavour.

Bake for 25 minutes or until the chips are cooked.

Notes

I mean, you could argue that they're just garlic and herb flavour, but, being on a healthy eating plan, 'garlic bread flavour' makes them sound and feel that much naughtier.

CREAMY GARLIC MASH

PREP TIME
5 minutes

COOK TIME
15 minutes

READY IN
20 minutes

SERVINGS
4 servings

CALORIES
190 Kcal serving

SOURCE
Sugar Pink Food

Ingredients

3 large potatoes, peeled and cut into cubes

½ garlic clove, grated

salt and pepper to taste

Steps

Boil the potatoes in a pan of water, until they have cooked and are soft.

Use a potato masher to crush and mash the potatoes.

Then use a normal whisk to whisk and whip the potatoes until they are completely smooth in texture. Add the garlic, salt and pepper.

Serve with plenty of vegetables and salad!

Notes

This creamy garlic mashed potato is so smooth, and so full of flavour!

HERBY WEDGES

PREP TIME
5 minutes

COOK TIME
35 minutes

READY IN
40 minutes

SERVINGS
4 servings

CALORIES
290 Kcal serving

SOURCE
Sugar Pink Food

Ingredients

1kg red-skinned potato, such as
Desiree

low calorie cooking spray

salt and pepper

1tsp smoked chilli powder

1tsp cayenne pepper

1tsp Italian herb seasoning

1tsp garlic salt

Steps

Mix together all the seasoning for the
wedges.

Line a baking tray with foil and place
the potato wedges, skin side down, on
the foil. Be sure to space evenly, so they
cook uniformly.

Spray with Frylight and sprinkle the
wedges seasoning over evenly.

Bake for 35 minutes, or until well
browned, crusty edged, and tender.

Notes
I love a herby wedge, they are so versatile and go well with almost anything!

SPICY RICE

PREP TIME
10 minutes

COOK TIME
20 minutes

READY IN
30 minutes

SERVINGS
1-2 people

CALORIES
401 Kcal serving

SOURCE
Sugar Pink Food

Ingredients

2 cups of brown rice

1 cup sweetcorn

1 stock cube

salt and pepper

1 onion diced

1 red pepper diced

1tbsp dried chilli

Steps

For the rice, fry-off the pepper, onion and sweet corn with Frylight in a pan.

Add 2 cups of rice to 4 cups of stock (made up using the stock cube). I used a coffee cup.

Bring to the boil and then simmer until all of the water is absorbed, which is usually around 20 minutes.

You'll need to stir it regularly to prevent it from sticking.

Notes
A tasty rice that is great on it's own, or as a side dish.

LIME & COCONUT RICE

PREP TIME
10 minutes

COOK TIME
20 minutes

READY IN
30 minutes

SERVINGS
4 servings

CALORIES
272 Kcal serving

SOURCE
Sugar Pink Food

Ingredients

250g jasmine rice

1tbsp desiccated coconut

juice of 1 lime

fresh coriander, roughly chopped

Steps

Boil the rice as per the pack instructions.

Add the coconut about 5 minutes before the end of the cooking time.

Drain the rice and then stir in the lime zest, juice, and coriander.

Notes
This rice is a perfect accompaniment for my Thai Chicken Strips!

OIL FREE ROAST POTATOES

PREP TIME
10 minutes

COOK TIME
45 minutes

READY IN
55 minutes

SERVINGS
4 servings

CALORIES
197 Kcal serving

SOURCE
Sugar Pink Food

Ingredients

As many potatoes as you can fit in your tray. Usually 3-4 potatoes

1 pint/570ml of hot stock. I use 2 stock cubes with the pint of water to make up the stock

low calorie cooking spray

Roast potato seasoning mix:

1tsp garlic powder

½tsp onion powder

1 stock cube, crumbled up

large pinch of salt and pepper

Steps

Peel the potatoes and chop to a medium roast potato size. Keep checking to make sure that there are enough for the roasting tin you are using. Preheat the oven to 190°C/gas mark 5. Par boil the potatoes for 5 minutes. Once cooked, drain the water away. Shake the pan to fluff the potatoes up.

Mix together the garlic powder, onion powder, crumbled up stock cube, salt and pepper. Sprinkle this over the potatoes, in the drained pan, and mix well to get an even coating. Add the potatoes to the roasting tin and pour the hot stock over the potatoes, ensuring they all get a covering. The stock should reach half way up the potatoes, to ensure perfect crispiness. Spray the tops of the potatoes with a generous amount of low calorie cooking spray, and add another pinch of salt and pepper.

Place them in the middle of the preheated oven. Add another spray of low calorie spray after 20 minutes. You will know the roast potatoes are ready because there will be no stock left in the tray and the potatoes will be crispy. I recommend keeping your eye on them during cooking. If the stock dries up too much, add a little more.

Notes
Perfect oil free roast potatoes that are crispy and delicious!

COLESLAW

PREP TIME
5 minutes

COOK TIME
0 minutes

READY IN
5 minutes

SERVINGS
4 servings

CALORIES
185 Kcal serving

SOURCE
Sugar Pink Food

Ingredients

2 carrots

1 cabbage

1 onion

1 apple

3tbsp of Quark

1tbsp fat free fromage frais

Steps

Shred all of the ingredients and mix in a bowl with salt and pepper.

Stir in the fromage frais and quark.

Put in a sealable container and keep in the fridge ready for salads.

Notes

A really simple side dish that is perfect for sandwiches and salads.

Easy Recipe Finder

Chicken recipes (continued)

Beef Recipes

Beef Recipes (Continued)

Pork Recipes

Lamb Recipes

Vegetarian Recipes

Vegetarian Recipes (Continued)

Meatball Recipes

Burger Recipes

Rice Dishes

CHICKEN & BACON DIRTY RICE 60

CHICKEN FRIED RICE 76

BBQ BURRITO BOWLS 83

EASY PAELLA 110

Soups

SWEET POTATO & CARROT SOUP 34

CREAM OF TOMATO SOUP 37

VEGETABLE SOUP 46

POTATO & LEEK SOUP 49

CHEESE TOASTIE & TOMATO SOUP 51

SLOW COOKER RAMEN NOODLE SOUP 89

Pasta Dishes

ITALIAN PASTA SALAD 35

BLT PASTA SALAD 40

PHILLY CHEESESTEAK PASTA 59

GARLIC CHICKEN & PROSCIUTTO PASTA 62

CREAMY PESTO PASTA 74

MEXICAN ENCHILADA LASAGNE 79

CREAMY TOMATO & CHICKEN PASTA 81

Printed in Great Britain
by Amazon

75089015R00078